Duologues

for all accents and ages

Eamonn Jones

and

Jean Marlow

A&C Black • London

To Kip and Annie

'*A Great Duo*'

Published in 1997
A & C Black (Publishers) Limited
35 Bedford Row, London WC1R 4JH

ISBN 0-7136-4766-3

A CIP catalogue record for this book is
available from the British Library.

Cover photograph by Michael Ward of Patricia Routledge and James
Simmons in *The Rivals*. Reproduced with the kind permission of P.A.L.

Typeset in 10 on 12 pt Sabon by Florencetype Ltd, Stoodleigh, Devon
Printed in Great Britain by Redwood Books, Trowbridge, Wilts

Contents

Acknowledgements ix

Foreword 1

In Your Own Time 2

   Ian Pettitt 2
   Administrator and Programmer, The Actors'
   Centre

   Dr Diana Devlin 3
   Head of Drama Studies, Guildhall School of Music
   and Drama

Advice on Some of the Selections 5

   Tom Stoppard 5
   Playwright

   April de Angelis 6
   Playwright

   Jonathan Cecil 6
   Actor

   Frances Cuka 7
   Actress

   Michael Attenborough 7
   Principal Associate Director,
   Royal Shakespeare Company

   Yvonne Brewster 8
   Artistic Director, Talawa Theatre Company

   Don Taylor 9
   Theatre and television director; playwright

   Carol Schroder 10
   Examiner, London Academy of Music and Dramatic
   Art (LAMDA)

The Duologues (see detailed contents on vi–viii) 11

Copyright Holders 164

Duologues for Two Men

Another Country.................. Julian Mitchell.................. 12

Art... Yasmina Reza; translated
by Christopher Hampton 16

Blood Knot .... Athol Fugard.................. 21

Daughters of Venice .... Don Taylor...................... 25

Dead Dad Dog.................... John McKay..................... 29

Dr Faustus .... Christopher Marlowe....... 33

The Herbal Bed .... Peter Whelan 36

An Ideal Husband............... Oscar Wilde..................... 39

The Importance of
Being Earnest .... Oscar Wilde..................... 41

On the Ledge...................... Alan Bleasdale 44

Plunder................................ Ben Travers 47

Sleuth................................... Anthony Shaffer.............. 51

Someone Who'll Watch
Over Me............................... Frank McGuinness........... 54

Up 'n' Under....................... John Godber..................... 58

The Witch of Edmonton ..... William Rowley, Thomas
Dekker and John Ford..... 63

Duologues for Two Women

Back to Methuselah	Bernard Shaw	66
The Beaux' Stratagem	George Farquhar..............	69
Bold Girls	Rona Munro....................	72
Borderline.............................	Hanif Kureishi	75
Green Forms	Alan Bennett....................	78
Have You Seen Zandile?	Gcina Mhlope, Maralin Vanrenen and Thembi Mtshali	82
An Ideal Husband...............	Oscar Wilde.....................	86
The Killing of Sister George	Frank Marcus	89
Kindertransport	Diane Samuels	93
Les Liaisons Dangereuses	Christopher Hampton	96
Playhouse Creatures.............	April de Angelis..............	100
The Positive Hour...............	April de Angelis..............	104
The Shoemaker's Holiday	Thomas Dekker	107
The Steamie..........................	Tony Roper	110
Stevie	Hugh Whitemore	113

Duologues for One Man and One Woman

Amadeus	Peter Shaffer	117
Bar Mitzvah Boy	Jack Rosenthal	120
The Crucible	Arthur Miller	124
Dirty Linen and New-Found-Land	Tom Stoppard	127
An Echo in the Bone	Dennis Scott	130
Indian Ink	Tom Stoppard	134
Love for Love	William Congreve	137
Measure for Measure	William Shakespeare	140
Once a Catholic	Mary O'Malley	144
The Playboy of the Western World	J.M. Synge	147
Pride and Prejudice	Jane Austen; adapted by Sue Pomeroy	150
The Rivals	Richard Brinsley Sheridan	153
Spend, Spend, Spend	Jack Rosenthal	156
Under Milk Wood	Dylan Thomas	159
When We Are Married	J.B. Priestley	161

Acknowledgements

We would like to say thank you to the actors, directors, producers, playwrights and organisations who have helped us with this book including:

Brian Schwartz of Offstage Bookshop, Gillian Diamond Associate Producer of the Peter Hall Company, Helen Fry, Mark Dobson, Sue Parrish of the Sphinx Company, Ian Pettitt of The Actors' Centre, Dr Diana Devlin, Eric Hollis and Geoffrey Salter of the Guildhall School of Music and Drama, Carol Schroder of the London Academy of Music and Dramatic Art, Michael Attenborough, Ed Berman, Yvonne Brewster, Jonathan Cecil, Frances Cuka, April de Angelis, Serena Dilnot, Rona Laurie, Jacky Matthews, Keith Salberg, Marie Shine, Tom Stoppard, Jane Tassell and Don Taylor.

Also students from The Actors' Theatre School who workshopped these duologues:

Aviva Adda, Athos Antoniades, Tay Brandon, Jennifer Crosdale, Kevin Daly, John Driscoll, Georgina Ford, Beverley Hance, John Higgins, Josephine Inoniyegha, Oliver Johnson, Tina Moran, Beatrice Schokkaert, Amieth Yogarajah.

And not forgetting our indefatigable Editor, Tesni Hollands.

Foreword

It is refreshing to know that the compilers of this selection of duologues are working actors, as well as being Directors of The Actors' Theatre School. Jean Marlow and Eamonn Jones are therefore particularly well qualified for this task both because of their practical experience in the professional theatre and their involvement with the training of students.

They realise what valuable use may be made of duologues in the course of actor training; a resource which is often overlooked. Short scenes involving two performers playing roles of equal importance provide drama students with the opportunity to get concentrated experience in a short space of time: both actors are fully involved during rehearsals and each is made aware of those important acting skills – listening and reacting. The duologue is a bridge between solo and ensemble work.

Apart from its usefulness to drama students, *Duologues for all accents and ages* is a useful source of material for those taking National Curriculum and Theatre Studies examinations and Speech and Drama examinations generally.

Duologue classes are among the most popular in the Speech and Drama section of Festivals affiliated to the British Federation. As an adjudicator I have noticed that shared responsibility in a scene usually reduces the nervous tension in both performers.

This book provides a stimulating challenge and will be of practical use to actors, students, examinees and Festival entrants as well as to teachers and drama tutors.

Rona Laurie
FGSM, LRAM, GODA, FRSA

In Your Own Time

'Would you like to read this scene for us? ... In your own time ... Mandy, our ASM, will read in the other part ...' The moment has come! You have managed to get an audition. The director or casting director has hopefully had 'a little chat' explaining the play, the story-line and some background of the character you hope to be playing. Mandy, now familiar with her part, is ready to devour the script. For better or worse you are involved in a 'duologue'. Can you pick up on the lines? Are you lifting them off the page? Are you engaging Mandy in eye contact? Is your characterisation approximating the playwright's intention? You may be winning if the director asks you to read another scene and gives you some further directions.

An audition scenario like this is going to be a vital part of your life as an actor and it is as well to consider whether you are giving yourself every chance to be at the point of preparation that turns opportunity into success. As part of your daily routine of relaxation, voice and movement exercises and sight-reading (You don't? Not even twenty minutes a day? – I didn't hear that!) a dip into the duologues is perhaps that little extra stimulation you need to bring your skills to a defined performance level, as you explore the plays and characters you might be called upon to play sooner than you think!

Ian Pettitt, Administrator and Programmer at the vibrant Actors' Centre, considers that duologues are a 'must' in their workshops for professional actors:

> If you are only doing monologues you have thirteen people just sitting around watching. Duologues are much more useful and informative and give twice as many people a chance to be involved. After all, ninety per cent of your time on stage will be spent talking to other people, not standing there on your own.

Nowadays drama schools presenting their final year showcases, to which agents and casting directors are invited, include an evening or afternoon of duologues and monologues as well as

2

the usual full-length play. This means that each student has a chance to show themselves in a leading role, whereas, in a play, inevitably some students will be stuck with a part that is either too old for them, or is so small that nobody is going to notice them. The old adage, 'There are no small parts, only small actors', is often only an excuse for 'Sorry, there weren't enough parts to go round'!

Duologues in performance examinations

Duologues are increasing in popularity among students entering for acting examinations, such as those held at the Guildhall School of Music and Drama and the London Academy of Music and Dramatic Art (LAMDA). Duo partners are marked individually and solo candidates may also enter with a partner, who will need to learn the lines but is *not* being examined. The time limit allowed for each section is between four and seven minutes, depending on the grade being taken. Choice is important and in the earlier grades the two duologues presented should be well contrasted. As students progress towards diploma level they will need to find scenes from contrasting periods, such as Elizabethan, Jacobean and eighteenth century. In our selections we have assumed *both* partners will be being examined and we have tried to include only those scenes where both characters share the dialogue and/or are of equal importance.

Dr Diana Devlin, MA (Cantab), PhD, is Head of Drama Studies at the Guildhall School of Music and Drama, and is also on the Board of Directors of Shakespeare's Globe on Bankside. She had this to say:

> Everyone who has to do an audition speech knows that performing on your own can be a thankless task. Acting really begins when you're in a scene, and you have to listen and respond to what's going on. In a duologue, it's not just your own performance you have to worry about – you also have to support your partner. Funnily enough, that often leads to the best acting of all.
> In North America, I have watched undergraduates who had to put together an acting 'recital' as part of their degree.

3

They would ask friends and colleagues to take part in scenes with them. Some of the most moving performances I saw were by their friends, because they were acting out of *generosity*.

This book is a good introduction to acting with a partner. If you like one of the duologues, the first thing to do is to read the whole play. Only when you know your character, and how he or she fits into the play as a whole, can you begin to bring the scene to life.

Duologues in the drama section of festivals

Here again the duologue classes in the Speech and Drama section are very popular indeed and choice is important. It is wise to look for a scene that has not been used year after year and make sure that it is suitable for your age and capabilities. It is often a good idea to give a short introduction so that the adjudicator and audience know what the scene is about and what has led up to a particular 'meeting' or 'confrontation'. The time limit in each class is usually about five minutes.

In both examinations and festivals the time limit is most important and should be strictly adhered to, otherwise you may either be stopped mid-scene or marked down if your duologue overruns.

The length of duologues in this book varies, and each should be timed carefully. Very few run over five minutes, but when you read the play you will see that a scene often continues – as in the *Green Forms* selection – for another two or three minutes and can be lengthened to meet examination or festival requirements. You should also take into account the amount of 'business' in a scene which doesn't appear to have much dialogue – as in the Phipps and Lord Goring 'buttonhole' scene from *An Ideal Husband*. Timing can alter quite alarmingly once you start running a piece.

Advice on Some of the Selections

We have invited well-known playwrights, actors, directors and an examiner to talk about scenes from plays which they have either written, played in, directed or examined.

Tom Stoppard is one of our busiest playwrights. His earlier plays include, amongst others, *Rosencrantz and Guildenstern are Dead*, *Jumpers*, *Travesties*, and *Dirty Linen and New-Found-Land*, an Ambiance Lunch-Hour Theatre Club presentation first staged at Inter-Action's tiny Almost Free Theatre in April 1976.

> *Dirty Linen* was supposed to be a play to celebrate [director] Ed Berman's British Naturalisation, but it went off into a different direction – *New-Found-Land* was then written to re-introduce the American Connection.

The play opened at the Arts Theatre three months later to enthusiastic reviews. *The Times* called it 'hilariously funny' and the *Guardian* talked of 'Puns, paradoxes, misunderstandings and double bluffs' that 'pour out like quicksilver ...'. Clarity of diction was essential in these fast-moving scenes, where styles shift rapidly from sophisticated comedy over to music hall.

> Many a laugh is lost because an audience hasn't heard the important line, or in some cases the 'build-up' to it. The scene between Maddie and Cocklebury-Smythe (reproduced in this book) gathers momentum as it moves along, but it still has to be precise. Maddie is described as being good at tongue twisters, but we need to hear every word she says, especially as she is setting up a 'running gag' that is to continue through to the end of the first act.
>
> During the run of *Dirty Linen* I'd come across actors sitting around in the theatre bar holding post-mortems on the night's performance, and agonising about not being able to get laughs on particular lines – should they come in on the line a bit quicker, pause a bit longer, change an inflection – when most of the time, as I kept telling them, all they needed was to make themselves heard!

April de Angelis' most recent plays include *Hush* at the Royal Court Theatre, London in 1992 and *The Positive Hour* at Hampstead Theatre in 1997. *Playhouse Creatures* was first performed at the Haymarket Studio, Leicester in 1993 and opened later at the Lyric Studio, Hammersmith the same year, following a national tour, and directed by Sue Parrish. It was later produced by the Peter Hall Company.

> *Playhouse Creatures* was originally commissioned and produced by the Sphinx Theatre Company. One of the specifications was for an all-female cast of five. In Scene Two I wanted to put across the sense of a society which, due to the upheavals of Civil War and plague, had had its old patterns disrupted and now allowed a space for change for women, in the theatre at least. Mrs Farley is a 'repressed' character who finds an opportunity for change in cheating on the more free-spirited, generous Nell. I suppose the scene needs the actors to trace Mrs Farley's change of mind and also to allow for the penny to drop in Nell's mind believably.
>
> There's a fair bit of setting up to be done in this scene. It starts *in situ* and challenges the actors to create the sort of energy which will involve and interest the audience at the start of the play.

Jonathan Cecil graduated from Oxford, trained at LAMDA and has appeared in many West End plays. He has co-starred in numerous television comedy series and played Hastings to Peter Ustinov's Poirot.

> When, years ago, I was asked to play Phipps in *An Ideal Husband* at the Oxford Festival I had misgivings – what could I do with such a small part? In fact it is among the most rewarding of cameo roles: with the right inscrutable, all-knowing dignity, Phipps can and perhaps should discreetly dominate the third act.
>
> Playing a butler is for an actor a marvellous exercise in *listening*; just listening, never reacting. The master, Lord Goring, a celebrated wit, clearly tries out his *bons mots* on his manservant. Whether Phipps finds them amusing or foolish or a bit of both is for the player to decide but never indicate either facially or verbally. Each 'Yes, m'lord' or 'No, m'lord' should be delivered in the same impeccably polite but impassive tone.

The 'buttonhole' scene is leisurely. Wilde's witticisms unlike, say, Noël Coward's must be spoken slowly enough for an audience to savour them. But the cues should be picked up without the slightest hesitation – until the pause indicated by Wilde himself after Phipps voices his own spontaneous opinion, about the lower class losing their relations. This should get a big laugh. There is never any eye contact between the two men but there must be perfect teamwork; as in the removing of Goring's hat, cape and stick and the presentation of the buttonhole: calm, smooth and stylish.

These adjectives epitomise the partnership between effervescent master and phlegmatic servant: they are united by an equal devotion to pure style.

Frances Cuka, Royal Shakespeare and Royal National Theatre actress, who has appeared in many Restoration comedies, talks about *The Beaux' Stratagem.*

In ladies' loos, the world over, women congregate to repair their make-up and talk about men. In this female bastion, a fly on the wall is bound to hear, 'What's he like?', 'Do you fancy him?', 'What did he say?', 'Or do?' Eyebrows are raised, eyes roll, amid gusts of giggling. Maybe not as witty as Dorinda and Mrs Sullen, but sisters under the skin.

And as sometimes happens with the modern counterparts, so their banter suddenly touches a nerve – while Dorinda is free to imagine herself Lady Aimwell, Mrs Sullen is a married woman tied to an unloved and unloving husband. She is falling in love with a man she believes to be a penniless servant, and she has no money of her own. In those days a woman couldn't get out of a bad marriage, for any property she might have owned prior to that marriage usually became the property of her husband, to do with it as he pleased. Even her clothes were his.

In the end Mrs Sullen decides to divorce her unpleasant husband, and gets her money back, but at this time in the play, happiness seems an impossible dream. But love has been kindled, and it brings the hope that something can be done to change her lot.

Michael Attenborough, Principal Associate Director of the Royal Shakespeare Company, directed *The Herbal Bed* at The

Other Place, Stratford in 1996. It moved to The Pit in the Barbican Theatre and transferred to the Duchess Theatre in April 1997.

> As will be clear, even to those who have not read the whole play, this scene is a test. John is a distinguished Stratford physician testing a young lad who is working for him as an apprentice doctor. Jack doesn't really want to take up the medical profession and is merely undergoing the training in order to satisfy his father and hence hold on to his allowance.
>
> John is a devoted doctor and a committed puritan. Jack is the second son of a wealthy landed gentry family. He is bright, charming and witty but crucially flawed – lazy, frequently drunk and lecherous.
>
> John is near the end of his patience with him. He is acutely aware that Jack doesn't really want to be there and is wasting his time. However, he is a fair man and is giving Jack every chance to redeem himself. This is a crucial moment for Jack as he needs to succeed in this test in order to convince John to continue to teach him and thus enable him to keep his father's allowance. John maintains the formality and precision of an oral examination. Jack is doing all he can to please his examiner. Both men have clearly distinct and different objectives.
>
> PS Jack is written with a Warwickshire accent in mind, albeit not particularly strong.

Yvonne Brewster, OBE, Artistic Director of Talawa Theatre Company, directed *An Echo in the Bone* at the Drill Hall in London in 1986.

> The author states that all characters are black. It is however immediately clear that some of the characters will have to play white parts.
>
> One of the most interesting and challenging aspects of our rehearsal period was the process by which we dealt with black people playing white parts. Much has been written on white actors blacking up to play Othello, but the reverse notion had never been so hotly discussed. We had to. So were we going to white up? The derisory laughter which greeted that suggestion from one unsuspecting actor spoke volumes. If white men must not black up to play black men

then the other way round was even more ridiculous. The Black and White Minstrels loomed.

We experimented with masks but that was unsatisfactory as it lacked subtlety. The masks could also be mistaken for a clumsy way of doubling; in other words it could have been interpreted that, not having enough money to pay the white actors, we used the black. Anyway by doing that we felt we would have failed the author in a most fundamental way.

We then spent a lot of time looking at the physicality of the text and that led us to the physicality of race and the movement of the various periods which the script addresses. The task was to put all the elements together. We felt this process enabled us to answer some of the questions that, as Dennis Scott said, lie deep in the racial memory – as an echo in the bone.

Don Taylor, well-known theatre and television director and playwright (there is a selection from his play *Daughters of Venice* in this book) directed *The Crucible* for BBC Television in 1981.

Pay attention to the language. Miller has created a unique theatrical language for his American Puritans which convinces as seventeenth-century speech while remaining entirely modern and capable of expressing current dilemmas. It is as much theatre poetry as any in modern English, and nothing at all to do with naturalistic speech, only the apparent imitation and enrichment of such speech. Its purpose is to contain the great emotional intensity of the scene, and the actors should use it to release the profound and savage passions it contains.

It is not necessary to use an American accent if you don't want to, and you should not let that consideration constrict your acting. How American Puritans spoke is guesswork: hardly any of them were more than one generation from England, and some were native English immigrants. It is more important to make Miller's poetry work than imitate modern American accents.

The excerpt is the great climax of a long, slowly developing scene, in which buried emotions are gradually revealed in all their nakedness. Thus the climax alone is hard to act. Somehow, the actors must attempt to imply what has led up to this great moment of revelation.

Carol Schroder, LLAM is an Examiner for the London Academy of Music and Dramatic Art (LAMDA) and an experienced teacher of Drama and Performing Arts. She is the author of several textbooks.

The authors have researched a diverse and exciting collection of scenes, many of which meet the requirements demanded by various Performing Arts courses and in particular the LAMDA examinations.

As a teacher I especially enjoyed the demands and challenges presented by the scene from *Bar Mitzvah Boy*; here both characters were well balanced, giving each student equal opportunity to develop their roles and to explore the background and style of the play. It might be interesting to study the importance of the Bar Mitzvah ceremony to the Jewish culture.

In complete contrast Derek and Mary Mooney's scene from *Once a Catholic* offers excellent opportunities for the student to study dialect and enjoy Mary O'Malley's humorous text where timing is of the essence. Here, looking at the Fifties culture of the Teddy Boys, with their distinctive clothing and lifestyle, would be well worth while.

As an examiner I am always delighted to commend originality of choice where appropriate and the duologues in this book provide a valuable contribution to students and teachers alike when preparing a balanced and well-contrasted programme for performance.

The Duologues

GUY BENNETT   TOMMY JUDD
17   17

Another Country
Julian Mitchell

First produced at the Greenwich Theatre in 1981 and then transferred to the Queens Theatre, Shaftesbury Avenue.

The play is set in an English public school in the early
Thirties, where future leaders of the ruling class are being
prepared for their entry into the Establishment. In this envi-
ronment the two main characters, Guy Bennett, coming to
terms with his homosexuality, and Tommy Judd, a committed
Marxist, are very much 'outsiders'.

This scene is set in the library at night. Judd, dressed in
pyjamas, is reading by a shaded light. There is a scrabbling
sound and Bennett, dressed in tails and a fancy waistcoat,
appears at the window, having climbed up the drainpipe.

Published by Amber Lane Press, Oxford

Act One, Scene Four

BENNETT [*off, in a loud whisper*] Hell!

[*Judd waits a moment, then pounces as Bennett is half in and
half out of the window.*]

JUDD [*imitating Fowler, in a low whisper*] All right, Bennett! I've
got you this time!

[*For a moment Bennett thinks it really is Fowler. Then he
relaxes and hauls himself in. He is wearing tails, fancy waistcoat and buttonhole, just like a member of Twenty Two.*]

BENNETT God, I thought you were Fowler!

JUDD Ssh! What on earth are you doing?

BENNETT Celebrating!

JUDD But I thought you didn't have to be back till tomorrow
morning.

BENNETT [*brushing himself down*] That drainpipe's a bloody
disgrace. Someone should have a word with Farcical.

JUDD Ssh!

BENNETT Tommy – may I call you Tommy, Tommy?

JUDD If you want.

BENNETT Tommy – I'm in love.

JUDD That's not exactly news.

BENNETT I don't mean 'in love', I mean *in love*.

JUDD You're drunk.

BENNETT It's *like* being drunk. Only instead of things going round and round, they're perfectly, beautifully still. And not blurred – sharp – clear – brighter colours than you've ever seen. It's – it's unbelievable.

JUDD The wedding was a success, then.

BENNETT It wasn't a wedding. More – an engagement party.

JUDD What? But—

BENNETT Oh, you mean the *wedding*! That was *ghastly*. Mother blubbed. And Arthur – he wants me to call him *Arthur*, can you believe it?

JUDD Perhaps it's his name.

BENNETT I told her – *you* can call him anything you like, he's *your* husband, I shall call him Colonel, and that's that.

JUDD Ssh!

BENNETT Leaving me to rot in this jail of a school, while she flaunts herself up and down the Riviera with that – that—

JUDD *Ssh!*

BENNETT Sorry, but – I mean, really! It's so undignified, people that age going off to Cap Ferrat. They should creep down to Cromer, and think themselves lucky. Tweeds and plus-fours and out on the links all day – that's what they should be doing. I told them so. Made mother blub *again*.

JUDD Cad!

BENNETT But they're trying to get rid of me, Tommy! They've got a world tour all set up – Cape Town, Singapore, Hong Kong – *Australia*! I ask you!

JUDD Really!

BENNETT It's the Martineau business. They fear for my moral character.

JUDD Bit late for that, isn't it?

BENNETT You must be mad, I said. I'm not leaving *now*. School's just getting to the good bit.

JUDD I didn't know there was a good bit.

BENNETT Oh, well, for you there isn't. You're determined not to have one. But for sensible people – *me* – I'm going to dress like this every day next term, Tommy.

JUDD [*dry*] You'll have to be careful not to get any more food on the waistcoat, then. It's grubby already.

BENNETT Damn the waistcoat. I've been waiting for this ever since my first day at prepper.

JUDD How pathetic.

BENNETT Nothing'll be as good again till I'm Ambassador in Paris.

JUDD Childish.

BENNETT Life is ladders. That's all. Prepper to here. First form to sixth. Second assistant junior Under-secretary to Ambassador in Paris. Ladders and love. It's so wonderful being in love.

JUDD So you said.

BENNETT I took James to dinner at the 'Fox and Hounds'.

JUDD [*baffled*] Who's James?

BENNETT Harcourt. His name's James. [*He has difficulty saying it.*] His name is James.

JUDD You're mad!

BENNETT We arranged it all yesterday. If my mother was marrying *Arthur*, I didn't see why I shouldn't have dinner with James. He told his House Man his uncle was coming down. [*sudden thought*] I am a fool. I should have booked a room.

JUDD [*thinking it's just another story*] Why not the bridal suite?

BENNETT [*serious*] No. No, that would have spoiled it. And anyway, he had to be in by nine-thirty. We wouldn't have had time.

JUDD My God! You really did go!

BENNETT You know, till now, it's all just been a game. Manoeuvring for glances, meeting accidentally-on-purpose. It was simply relieving the boredom. But now—

JUDD You'll be sunkered.

BENNETT No, no.

JUDD Masters drink at the 'Fox and Hounds' [*Bennett shrugs.*] Bennett, you *are* mad.

BENNETT [*picking up the binoculars*] Do call me Guy. It's so stupid, surnames. Have you ever really been in love?

JUDD No.

BENNETT It's— [*Pause.*] I've been walking about. Thinking. What time is it now?

JUDD Getting on for one.

BENNETT Three hours!

JUDD Why didn't you come back here?

BENNETT Because I've got an exeat. I'm free! I'm not here at all, I'm in London!

JUDD Ssh, for God's sake! You'll get us both beaten!

BENNETT They can't beat me if I'm not here!

[*He laughs.*]

JUDD *Ssh!*

BENNETT I think I'll sleep in here, if you don't mind.

JUDD You'd better not let anyone find you dressed like that. You'll get the gamut for that waistcoat.

BENNETT [*stretching out on the window-seat*] When I'm in Twenty Two I'll have a fag to keep it clean. Everything will be absolutely— [*He yawns.*] Oh, Tommy! *Amor vincit omnia!*

JUDD You're hopeless. A totally hopeless case.

BENNETT Don't worry about me. I shan't disturb you. I'm asleep already.

[*Pause.*]

JUDD Do you honestly think this is wise? [*Pause.*] If you're really *not* drunk, I do think— [*Pause.*] Oh, well, it's nothing to do with me.

BENNETT Bliss!

JUDD First they take away my torches. Then, when I take my life, or at least my bum, in my hands, and creep down here – they send me *you*. This place is impossible!

[*He switches off the light.*]

BENNETT [*drowsy*] Good night!

JUDD Good night!

[*He goes. Pause. Then Bennett begins to sing 'Who stole my heart away'. He rises. He begins to dance.*]

YVAN   MARC

Art

Yasmina Reza
Translated by Christopher Hampton

First produced at the Comédie des Champs-Elysées, Paris in 1994 and in this translation at Wyndhams Theatre, London in 1996.

The action takes place in the main room of a flat, the scenes unfolding successively at Serge's, Yvan's and Marc's. Nothing changes except the painting on the wall.

Serge has bought a modern painting for a great deal of money. Marc strongly disapproves of the purchase, questioning his friend's obsession for a white canvas with white lines on it. The once valued friendship becomes more and more strained as Yvan tries to placate them both, only succeeding in making matters worse.

This scene opens in Yvan's flat. Yvan is crawling on all fours looking for the top of his felt-tip pen. He turns to introduce himself to the audience. Marc enters and starts to help him in his search. The conversation turns to Serge and the disputed 'picture'.

Published by Faber & Faber, London

Act One

YVAN I'm Yvan.

I'm a bit tense at the moment, because, having spent my life in textiles, I've just found a new job as a sales agent for a wholesale stationery business.

People like me. My professional life has always been a failure and I'm getting married in a couple of weeks. She's a lovely intelligent girl from a good family.

[*Marc enters. Yvan has resumed his search and has his back to him.*]

MARC What are you doing?

YVAN I'm looking for the top of my pen.

[*Time passes.*]

MARC All right, that's enough.

YVAN I had it five minutes ago.

MARC It doesn't matter.

YVAN Yes, it does.

[*Marc gets down on his knees to help him look. Both of them spend some time looking. Marc straightens up.*]

MARC Stop it. Buy another one.

YVAN It's a felt-tip, they're special, they'll write on any surface ... It's just infuriating. Objects, I can't tell you how much they infuriate me. I had it in my hand five minutes ago.

MARC Are you going to live here?

YVAN Do you think it's suitable for a young couple?

MARC Young couple! Ha, ha ...

YVAN Try not to laugh like that in front of Catherine.

MARC How's the stationery business?

YVAN All right. I'm learning.

MARC You've lost weight.

YVAN A bit. I'm pissed off about that top. It'll all dry up. Sit down.

MARC If you go on looking for that top, I'm leaving.

YVAN OK, I'll stop. You want something to drink?

MARC A Perrier, if you have one.

Have you seen Serge lately?

YVAN No. Have you?

MARC Yesterday.

YVAN Is he well?

MARC Very.

He's just bought a painting.

YVAN Oh yes?

MARC Mm.

YVAN Nice?

MARC White.

YVAN White?

MARC White.

Imagine a canvas about five foot by four ... with a white background ... completely white in fact ... with fine white diagonal stripes ... you know ... and maybe another horizontal white line, towards the bottom ...

YVAN How can you see them?

MARC What?

YVAN These white lines. If the background's white, how can you see the lines?

MARC You just do. Because I suppose the lines are slightly grey, or vice versa, or anyway there are degrees of white! There's more than one kind of white!

YVAN Don't get upset. Why are you getting upset?

MARC You immediately start quibbling. Why can't you let me finish?

YVAN All right. Go on.

MARC Right. So, you have an idea of what the painting looks like.

YVAN I think so, yes.

MARC Now you have to guess how much Serge paid for it.

YVAN Who's the painter?

MARC Antrios. Have you heard of him?

YVAN No. Is he fashionable?

MARC I knew you were going to ask me that!

YVAN Well, it's logical ...

MARC No, it isn't logical ...

YVAN Of course it's logical, you ask me to guess the price, you know very well the price depends on how fashionable the painter might be ...

MARC I'm not asking you to apply a whole set of critical standards, I'm not asking you for a professional valuation, I'm asking you what you, Yvan, would give for a white painting tarted up with a few off-white stripes.

YVAN Bugger all.

MARC Right. And what about Serge? Pick a figure at random.

YVAN Ten thousand francs.

MARC Ha!

YVAN Fifty thousand.

MARC Ha!

YVAN A hundred thousand.

MARC Keep going.

YVAN A hundred and fifty? Two hundred?!

MARC Two hundred. Two hundred grand.

YVAN No!

MARC Yes.

YVAN Two hundred grand?

MARC Two hundred grand.

YVAN Has he gone crazy?

MARC Looks like it.
  [*Slight pause.*]
YVAN All the same . . .
MARC What do you mean, all the same?
YVAN If it makes him happy . . . he can afford it . . .
MARC So that's what you think, is it?
YVAN Why? What do you think?
MARC You don't understand the seriousness of this, do you?
YVAN Er . . . no.
MARC It's strange how you're missing the basic point of this story. All you can see is externals. You don't understand the seriousness of it.
YVAN What is the seriousness of it?
MARC Don't you understand what this means?
YVAN Would you like a cashew nut?
MARC Don't you see that suddenly, in some grotesque way, Serge fancies himself as a 'collector'.
YVAN Well . . .
MARC From now on, our friend Serge is one of the great connoisseurs.
YVAN Bollocks.
MARC Well of course it's bollocks. You can't buy your way in that cheap. But that's what *he* thinks.
YVAN Oh, I see.
MARC Doesn't that upset you?
YVAN No. Not if it makes him happy.
MARC If it makes him happy. What's that supposed to mean? What sort of a philosophy is that, if it makes him happy?
YVAN As long as it's not doing any harm to anyone else . . .
MARC But it is. It's doing harm to me! I'm disturbed, I'm disturbed, more than that, I'm hurt, yes, I am, I'm fond of Serge, and to see him let himself be ripped off and lose every ounce of discernment through sheer snobbery . . .
YVAN I don't know why you're so surprised. He's always haunted galleries in the most absurd way, he's always been an exhibition freak.
MARC He's always been a freak, but a freak with a sense of humour. You see, basically, what really upsets me is that you can't have a laugh with him any more.
YVAN I'm sure you can.
MARC You can't!
YVAN Have you tried?

MARC Of course I've tried. I laughed. Heartily. What do you think I did? He didn't crack a smile.

Mind you, two hundred grand, I suppose it might be hard to see the funny side.

YVAN Yes.

[*They laugh.*]

I'll make him laugh.

MARC I'd be amazed. Any more nuts?

YVAN He'll laugh, you just wait.

MORRIS   ZACHARIAH
South African   South African

Blood Knot
Athol Fugard

First performed at the Rehearsal Room (African Music and Drama Association), Johannesburg, South Africa in 1961 and in the UK at the New Victoria Theatre, Stoke-on-Trent in 1988.

The action takes place in a one-room shack in the 'non-white location' of Korsten, Port Elizabeth, occupied by two brothers – Morris, who is light-skinned and has some education, being able to read and write, and Zachariah, dark-skinned with no education.

The play explores the obsession with race and colour in South Africa and its effect on the lives of the two men, 'who were going to try to live without hope, without appeal'. After a year of only each other for company, Zachariah announces that he must have 'Woman'. Morris suggests he gets himself a pen-pal and together they search through advertisements, finally settling for a 'Miss Ethel Lange ... eighteen years old and well developed'.

In this scene, Zachariah has just returned from the Post Office and is sitting on his bed with one foot in a footbath prepared by Morris.

Published in *Selected Plays*, Athol Fugard, by Oxford University Press, Oxford

Scene Three

ZACHARIAH When your feet are bad, you feel it, man.

[*Morris starts helping Zachariah take off his coat. At this point Morris finds an envelope in the inside pocket of Zachariah's coat. He examines it secretly. Zachariah broods on, one foot in the basin.*]

MORRIS Zach, did you stop by the Post Office on your way back?

ZACHARIAH *Ja.* There was a letter there.

MORRIS I know there was. [*Holding up the envelope*.] I just found it.

ZACHARIAH Good.

MORRIS What do you mean, 'good'?

ZACHARIAH Good, like 'okay'.

MORRIS [*excited and annoyed*] What's the matter with you?

ZACHARIAH What's the matter with me?

MORRIS This is your pen-pal. This is your reply from Ethel!

ZACHARIAH In Oudtshoorn.

MORRIS But Zach! You must get excited, man! Don't you want to know what she said?

ZACHARIAH Sure.

MORRIS Shall we open it then?

ZACHARIAH Why not!

MORRIS [*tears open the letter*] By God, she did it! She sent you a picture of herself.

ZACHARIAH [*first flicker of interest*] She did?

MORRIS So this is Ethel!

ZACHARIAH Morrie . . . ?

MORRIS Eighteen years . . . and fully . . . developed.

ZACHARIAH Let me see, man!

[*He grabs the photograph. The certainty and excitement fade from Morris's face. He is obviously perplexed by something.*] Hey! Not bad. Now that's what I call a goosie. Good for old Oudtshoorn. You don't get them like this over here. That I can tell you. Not with a watch! Pretty smart, too. Nice hair. Just look at those locks. And how's that for a wall she's standing against? Ever seen a wall like that, as big as that, in Korsten? I mean it's made of bricks, isn't it!

MORRIS [*snatching the photograph out of Zachariah's hand and taking it to the window where he has a good look.*] Zach, let me have another look at her.

ZACHARIAH Hey! What's the matter with you! It's my pen-pal, isn't it? It is!

MORRIS Keep quiet, Zach!

ZACHARIAH What's this 'keep quiet'?

[*Morris throws the photograph down on the bed and finds the letter, which he reads feverishly. Zachariah picks up the photograph and continues his study.*]

ZACHARIAH You're acting like you never seen a woman in your life. Why don't you get a pen-pal? Maybe one's not enough.

MORRIS [*having finished the letter, his agitation is now even more pronounced*] That newspaper, Zach. Where is that newspaper?

ZACHARIAH How should I know?

MORRIS [*anguished*] Think, man!

ZACHARIAH You had it. [*Morris is scratching around frantically.*] What's the matter with you tonight? Maybe you threw it away.

MORRIS No. I was keeping it in case ... [*Finds it.*] Thank God! Oh, please, God, now make it that I am wrong!

[*He takes a look at the newspaper, pages through it, and then drops it. He stands quite still, unnaturally calm after the frenzy of the previous few seconds.*]

You know what you done, don't you?

ZACHARIAH Me?

MORRIS Who was it, then? Me?

ZACHARIAH But what?

MORRIS Who wanted woman?

ZACHARIAH Oh. Me.

MORRIS Right. Who's been carrying on about Minnie, and Connie, and good times? Not me.

ZACHARIAH Morrie! What are you talking about?

MORRIS That photograph.

ZACHARIAH I've seen it.

MORRIS Have another look.

ZACHARIAH [*he does*] It's Ethel.

MORRIS Miss Ethel Lange to you!

ZACHARIAH Okay, I looked. Now what!

MORRIS Can't you see, man! Ethel Lange is a white woman!

[*Pause. They look at each other in silence.*]

ZACHARIAH [*slowly*] You mean that this Ethel ... here ...

MORRIS Is a white woman!

ZACHARIAH How do you know?

MORRIS Oh for God's sake, Zach – use your eyes. Anyway, that paper you bought was white. There's no news about our sort.

ZACHARIAH [*studying the photo*] Hey – you're right, Morrie. [*Delighted.*] You're damn well right. And this white woman has written to me, a *hot-not*, a *swartgat*. This white woman thinks I'm a white man. That I like!

[*Zachariah bursts into laughter. Morris jumps forward and snatches the photograph out of his hand.*]

Hey! What are you going to do?

MORRIS What do you think?

ZACHARIAH Read it.

MORRIS I'm going to burn it.

ZACHARIAH No!

MORRIS Yes.

ZACHARIAH [*jumps up and comes to grips with Morris who, after a short struggle, is thrown violently to the floor. Zachariah picks up the letter and the photograph. He stands looking down at Morris for a few seconds, amazed at what he has done.*] No, Morrie. You're not going to burn it, Morrie.

MORRIS [*vehemently*] Yes, burn the bloody thing! Destroy it!

ZACHARIAH But it's my pen-pal, Morris. Now, isn't it? Doesn't it say here: 'Mr Zachariah Pietersen'? Well, that's me ... isn't it? It is. My letter. You just don't go and burn another man's letter, Morrie.

MILORD   BODGER
mid-twenties   about 20

Daughters of Venice
Don Taylor

First produced by the Chiswick Youth Theatre in 1991
and then at the Wilde Theatre in 1993, the play is set in
eighteenth-century Venice.

Milord is a young Englishman, good-looking and good-
hearted, but stupid beneath his fashionable charm. He has just
come into his inheritance and is determined to spend as much
of it as he can in Venice, and hopefully find himself a 'sensual
Venetian beauty' at the same time. He is accompanied by his
servant, Bodger, who is energetic, keen and always helpful,
but not overburdened with brains.

This scene is set in a street in Venice, with several alleyways
leading into a small square. Milord enters looking for Bodger,
then exits up another alley just as Bodger enters from the alley
Milord has not looked down. This is repeated until at last
Milord and Bodger arrive on stage at the same time.

Published by Samuel French, London

Act One
MILORD Bodger!
BODGER Yes, sir?
MILORD Where are you?
BODGER Here I am, sir.
MILORD Whenever I look for you, you're not there.
BODGER I am now, sir.
MILORD What?
BODGER There. I mean here.
MILORD For a gentleman's man you leave a lot to be desired.
BODGER Surely not, sir?
MILORD Yes, you do.
BODGER I didn't know you desired gentlemen's men that much, sir.

MILORD Bodger, you're a good-hearted fellow, but you're useless. What are you?

BODGER A good-hearted fellow, sir.

MILORD What do you think of Venice?

BODGER Fine, if you like water.

MILORD Isn't it splendid?

BODGER And you don't mind getting your feet wet in the main road.

MILORD Magnificent?

BODGER And you don't drive coaches for a living. Good place for getting drowned though. I don't like all these alleys.

MILORD What's wrong with them?

BODGER Too narrow. Too dark. Too full of Italians.

MILORD Bodger, you are an Englishman and a Philistine. You have no love for art, and your natural reaction to anything foreign is to say if it was any good we'd have it in England.

BODGER Yes, sir. That makes sense.

MILORD But let me tell you, there is no city in the world like this one! When I came here on the Grand Tour, to finish off my education—

BODGER Did you finish it off, sir?

MILORD Completely!

BODGER Oh good.

MILORD I have never experienced a time of such sustained delight: and I've never experienced it since.

BODGER Oh, I am sorry to hear that, sir.

MILORD And now that I have come so unexpectedly into my inheritance, I couldn't wait to come back! Bodger, we have so much money, we can hardly put one leg in front of the other with the weight of it!

BODGER Really, sir? I hadn't noticed.

MILORD I was speaking metaphorically.

BODGER Oh well, you can't expect me to understand then. I don't speak metaphoric.

MILORD We are loaded, Bodger!

BODGER So what are you going to do, sir, with all this cash?

MILORD Do you know what I remember most, Bodger, from my last trip?

BODGER No sir. But I shouldn't think it's the sort of thing you can say in public.

MILORD I was here with a man who knew Venice well, and he took me down a certain street – how shall I describe it? At every doorway and window there were men and women with the most inviting looks on their faces. And they all kept coming out towards my friend, jabbering in Italian – which I didn't speak then – and pointing to me, and smiling!

BODGER Laughing, even . . .

MILORD I asked my companion, what were these people selling. And he turned to me and said, 'My friend, whatever you want, they're selling it!'

BODGER He didn't!

MILORD I tell you he did!

BODGER What did you buy?

MILORD Never you mind.

BODGER Can I buy some?

MILORD Bodger, I have never forgotten that moment, and now that I own most of Leicestershire, I have come back, to claim my Italian inheritance!

BODGER What are you going to buy, sir? You can tell me, I won't let on to a soul.

MILORD We are going to buy paintings, Bodger, and music!

BODGER You're not serious!

MILORD And wine, and pleasure, and all the glory of life!

BODGER Now you're talking, sir, that sounds more like it!

MILORD Most of all Bodger, we are going to buy a delightful, charming, sloe-haired, plum-eyed, peach-skinned, cherry-lipped, sensual Venetian beauty!

BODGER And then we'll eat her with cream.

MILORD The women here, Bodger, are like no other women on earth! I have never forgotten the women I met here! We shall buy the most charming girl in Venice, and take her back to England with us!

BODGER But what will Madam your wife say?

MILORD She won't say anything Bodger, because she won't know! She is my duty as a gentleman. But my little Venetian beauty will be my pleasure as a scoundrel!

[*They both roar with laughter.*]

BODGER Perhaps she won't want to be bought, sir? Most women I know don't.

MILORD In this city, Bodger, you can buy anything, if you have enough money. And I do! And of course, I won't *tell* her I've bought her. I shall woo her with all the charm I possess!

BODGER Oh, that'll be all right then.

MILORD And set her up in Venetian splendour in the West Wing.

My wife can't stand the West Wing, she never goes there: it's too long a walk. And there I shall have a Venetian mistress, all of my own!

BODGER Sounds fine, sir. So long as the girl will put up with it.

MILORD What do you mean, put up with it? What greater honour could any foreign woman aspire to than to be an Englishman's mistress? It's the crowning glory of her sex!

BODGER Well, sir, it sounds like we're going to have a very good holiday.

MILORD Carnival begins tomorrow, and we must get masks and cloaks and three-cornered hats, and prepare to enjoy ourselves, incognito.

BODGER Does that mean legally or illegally, sir?

MILORD It means Bodger, there's no difference! There is you, and there is this unknown beauty. You don't know who she is, and she doesn't know who you are, and neither of you cares!

BODGER I say that every time, but they always say no.

MILORD Not here they don't! The first thing, Bodger, is to get us in to the Cardinal's great assembly tonight, in his palace on the Grand Canal.

BODGER How do I do that, sir?

MILORD With money, Bodger, with money! What other way is there?

BODGER None that I know, sir. Where is the Grand Canal?

MILORD Just keep walking that way and you can't miss it!

BODGER After you then, sir. I haven't been to a good Cardinal's party in years . . .

ECK   WILLIE
24   late 50s
Scottish   Scottish

Dead Dad Dog

John McKay

First performed at the Traverse Theatre, Edinburgh in May 1988 and transferred to the Royal Court Theatre Upstairs, London.

Eck is described as a young aspiring media type, currently unemployed. Throughout the action he is dogged by the ghost of his dad, Willie – a dead Hoover salesman dressed in a flared Seventies suit. He is cheery but dour.

In the opening scene Eck has come down to breakfast, and is anticipating the successful outcome of his interview with BBC Scotland that morning. As he starts to eat his cornflakes he is interrupted by the appearance of Willie – his 'Dead Dad'.

Published in *Scot-Free: New Scottish Plays* by Nick Hern Books, London

Scene One
ECK Today.
    Hm. A wee bit dull.
    No matter. Hello birds. Hello back green. Hello pink tee-shirt on somebody's line.
    Today.
    Today's gonna be a good one. An I'll tell you why.
    Number one. I've got up. Thank you, God.
    Number two. After watchin most of my friends scurry south to weather the long winter of recession and repression, my efforts to hang on in the country where the action's at but the cash is not have finally been rewarded. That is, this morning I've landed an interview for a halfway decent job. At 10.30 a.m. BBC Scotland will be exposed to the irresistible charm and dynamic ideas of hotshot Alexander Dundee. By 10.45 I'll have ma own series.

[*Confidential.*]

Yesterday I got a card from ma pal Donald. Just started workin for a trendy newspaper in London. Says they're lookin for another writer. Says I should apply. Well I say ha ha no sell out.

Number three. M-hm, number three, tonight I'm meeting Roseanne. So if you hear a sound like a pneumatic drill, it's no Embra Corporation digging up the roads again – it's my heart saying to my brain, wise up greystuff, this girl makes me wanna play the bongos. Wah!

[*Watch.*]

9.15. Time enough to have some breakfast. But on a day like this, it's no just breakfast. It's hello cornflakes in yer bright square box, what a nice free gift you gave me last week, out you come, dinnae mind ma hand, and then hello milk chock full of calcium yum yum sploosh.

[*He bends over and listens to the bowl.*]

ECK No sound. Wrong brand. No matter. You're fresh and you're crunchy and today you are mine, you are indeed my . . .

[*Willie has appeared.*]

WILLIE Hello son.

[*Eck drops the bowl of cornflakes. Smash!*]

ECK Dad.

WILLIE Aye. Son.

ECK Dad.

[*Pause.*]

ECK [*extended amazement*] You . . . you . . . em . . . you're . . . deid.

WILLIE Oh aye. Right enough. But A wouldnae mind a cup of tea.

[*Eck double-takes and slaps himself. But Willie is still there.*]

ECK Em, Dad, I mean you are deid aren't you? I mean you've no just been hiding out in East Kilbride or somewhere, done a bunk, like?

WILLIE Oh no. A've been deid . . . oh . . . twelve year now. You should ken that. A saw yez at the funeral.

ECK You saw me at the funeral.

WILLIE Oh aye. [*Winks.*] A wis watchin.

ECK Like how? From in the coffin or what?

WILLIE Well sort of in and out. A hadnae gone upstairs yet, you see.

ECK To em Heaven?

WILLIE Oh aye. Heaven. Aye.

[*Pause.*]

ECK Well.

WILLIE Well what?

ECK Well what's it like?

WILLIE What's what like?

ECK Heaven.

WILLIE Oh. Fine. Fine. Rains a lot. Bit like Rothesay, really.

[*Pause.*]

ECK So ... why? I mean why?

WILLIE Am A here? Oh A don't know really. A'm a bit scunnered maself. I didn't put in for it or anythin.

ECK I see.

[*He turns forward.*]

Breakfast time and ma father's ghost is sitting in my kitchen and he says Heaven is a bit like Rothesay and he's scunnered as to why he's here seeing as how he didn't put in for it.

Get a grip, Alec. Wash yer face. Aye just go and wash yer face, eh?

[*Eck gets up and walks to the 'door'.*]

ECK I must be a wee bit nervy this morning. Seein ghosts. Make that a lot nervy.

[*But suddenly, as he gets to the threshold, both he and Willie are wracked with terrible stomach pain ...*]

BOTH Oooyah!

ECK Aw ma guts ...

[*Eck looks at Willie, puzzled, then he takes a step forward. The pain gets worse. He steps back. At a certain distance from Willie the pain stops.*]

ECK Aw ... oh.

[*Eck steps forward and backward a few times, then rounds on Willie.*]

ECK Ma God. You're real.

WILLIE Of course A'm real.

ECK So what is this? What is this? Are you doing this?

WILLIE Sit down. A'm daein nothin.

ECK You are. You bloody well are. You're doing some kind of spell aren't you, you're doing voodoo so I cannae get away from you ...

WILLIE Look A'm a ghost, A'm just a ghost, son, A'm no Ali Bongo. An' ma stomach went wild too. Anyway, what's it matter? We've got a lot of catching up tae do. We want tae stick the gether. An' we've got aw day ...

ECK [*blank*] All day . . .

    All day! It's ten to ten! And I've got a job interview at ten-thirty? And I'm not even dressed . . .

    [*He rushes to the door. The pain hits again.*]

BOTH Ooyah!

ECK Awwww . . . Dad. Dad stand up. Aye, now. Now walk towards me . . .

    [*Willie staggers towards Eck; at a certain distance the pain stops.*]

BOTH Aaaaah . . .

WILLIE Hey, that's good.

ECK Fine. Just fine. Just as long as we stick together we don't get the Vincent Price appendicitis.

    [*Willie embraces him.*]

WILLIE William and Alexander Dundee. Just like Pinky and Perky, eh? D'you no remember we used tae watch that on the . . .

ECK [*breaking the embrace*] Look Dad, I'm gonna be awful busy the day and . . .

WILLIE Yes.

ECK I mean it's em nice . . . a nice surprise an' that . . . but can't you see that with you around . . .

WILLIE What?

ECK Well, can't you just . . .

WILLIE See what?

    [*A pause. Eck waves his arms about in exasperation.*]

ECK I don't believe this.

FAUSTUS   MEPHASTOPHILIS
middle-aged   any age

Dr Faustus
Christopher Marlowe

Possibly first performed in 1594, several months after the playwright's assassination, and set in Germany.

Dr Faustus is a tragedy of damnation. Faustus sells his soul
to the Devil in return for twenty-four years of knowledge, pleasure and power. His is the sin of pride with its inevitable
downfall. At the beginning of the play we see Faustus sitting
discontented in his study. He has vast fame, knowledge and
popularity, but he is still only 'man'. He rejects his study of
law and medicine, which can only restore health not life, and
turns to magic.

In this scene he conjures up, or thinks he has conjured up
Mephastophilis, who appears in the shape of a Franciscan friar.

Published by A&C Black, London

Scene Three

MEPHASTOPHILIS Now Faustus, what would'st thou have me do?
FAUSTUS I charge thee wait upon me whilst I live,
    To do what ever Faustus shall command,
    Be it to make the moon drop from her sphere,
    Or the ocean to overwhelm the world.
MEPHASTOPHILIS I am a servant to great Lucifer,
    And may not follow thee without his leave;
    No more than he commands must we perform.
FAUSTUS Did not he charge thee to appear to me?
MEPHASTOPHILIS No, I came now hither of mine own accord.
FAUSTUS Did not my conjuring speeches raise thee? Speak!
MEPHASTOPHILIS That was the cause, but yet *per accidens*[1],
    For when we hear one rack[2] the name of God,
    Abjure the Scriptures, and his saviour Christ,
    We fly in hope to get his glorious soul,

Nor will we come, unless he use such means
Whereby he is in danger to be damned:
Therefore the shortest cut for conjuring
Is stoutly to abjure the Trinity,
And pray devoutly to the prince of hell.

FAUSTUS So Faustus hath already done, and holds this principle:
There is no chief but only Beelzebub,
To whom Faustus doth dedicate himself.
This word damnation terrifies not him,
For he confounds hell in Elysium:
His ghost be with the old philosophers.
But leaving these vain trifles of men's souls,
Tell me, what is that Lucifer thy lord?

MEPHASTOPHILIS Arch-regent and commander of all spirits.

FAUSTUS Was not that Lucifer an angel once?

MEPHASTOPHILIS Yes Faustus, and most dearly loved of God.

FAUSTUS How comes it then that he is prince of devils?

MEPHASTOPHILIS O, by aspiring pride and insolence,
For which God threw him from the face of heaven.

FAUSTUS And what are you that live with Lucifer?

MEPHASTOPHILIS Unhappy spirits that fell with Lucifer,
Conspired against our God with Lucifer,
And are for ever damned with Lucifer.

FAUSTUS Where are you damned?

MEPHASTOPHILIS In hell.

FAUSTUS How comes it then that thou art out of hell?

MEPHASTOPHILIS Why this is hell, nor am I out of it.
Think'st thou that I, who saw the face of God,
And tasted the eternal joys of heaven,
Am not tormented with ten thousand hells
In being deprived of everlasting bliss!
O Faustus, leave these frivolous demands,
Which strike a terror to my fainting soul.

FAUSTUS What, is great Mephastophilis so passionate
For being deprived of the joys of heaven?
Learn thou of Faustus manly fortitude,
And scorn those joys thou never shalt possess.
Go bear these tidings to great Lucifer,
Seeing Faustus hath incurred eternal death
By desperate thoughts against Jove's deity:
Say, he surrenders up to him his soul
So he will spare him four and twenty years,

Letting him live in all voluptuousness,
Having thee ever to attend on me,
To give me whatsoever I shall ask,
To tell me whatsoever I demand,
To slay mine enemies, and aid my friends,
And always be obedient to my will.
Go, and return to mighty Lucifer,
And meet me in my study at midnight,
And then resolve me of thy master's mind.
MEPHASTOPHILIS I will Faustus.
   [*Exit.*]
FAUSTUS Had I as many souls as there be stars
I'd give them all for Mephastophilis.
By him I'll be great emperor of the world,
And make a bridge through the moving air
To pass the ocean with a band of men;
I'll join the hills that bind the Afric shore,
And make that land continent to Spain,
And both contributory to my crown.
The emperor shall not live but by my leave,
Nor any potentate of Germany.
Now that I have obtained what I desire
I'll live in speculation of this art
Till Mephastophilis return again.

---

[1] *per accidens* only in appearance; what the conjuring represented was the real cause

[2] *rack* violate: 'take the name of the Lord in vain'

JOHN HALL   JACK LANE
young/middle-aged   young

The Herbal Bed
Peter Whelan

First performed by the Royal Shakespeare Company at The
Other Place, Stratford-upon-Avon in 1996 and later at the
Barbican Theatre, London, it transferred to the Duchess
Theatre, London in 1997.

The play is based on events that took place in the summer
of 1613, when William Shakespeare's daughter, Susanna,
married to John Hall, a respected physician of Stratford, was
publicly accused by her husband's young apprentice, Jack Lane,
of having a sexual liaison with a family friend.

In this early scene, John Hall is walking in the garden of
his home with Jack Lane and testing him on his knowledge
of medicinal herbs.

Published by Warner/Chappell Plays, London

Act One, Scene Two
JOHN Achillea millefolium?
  [*Jack works at it.*]
JACK Ha ... um ... millefolium ...
JOHN Yarrow.
JACK Yarrow! Yes! I was going to say yarrow.
JOHN Which parts do we use?
JACK Flowering stems.
JOHN How do we administer?
JACK As an infusion ...
JOHN For which conditions?
JACK The runs ...
JOHN Diarrhoea, yes ...
JACK Wind ... backward ...
JOHN And?
JACK The curse ... the courses ... women's complaint.

JOHN Irregular lunar evacuations. Learn the proper terms. You have a list. There's no alternative but to learn it. What would you say of Aconitum Napellus ... monkshood?

JACK [*promptly*] Poison.

JOHN Yes. Name me some poisonous plants.

JACK Ivy. Deadly Night Shade, Cuckoopint ...

JOHN I would prefer you to accompany the names with the Latin. But we'll let it pass for now ... go on.

JACK Black-berried briony, thornapple, larkspur ... except the flowers ... Christmas rose, henbane, yew ...

JOHN Yes ... you seem to know your poisons ...

[*Hall's tone implies an inordinate interest in this area. Jack grins.*]

JACK That was your first instruction to me, Dr Hall ... to know what we had to be careful with.

JOHN I'm well aware of it. You see, when you came to me I thought you might have the usual problem that most have ... of applying the mind ... of concentration ... of absorbing knowledge. But it may not lie exactly there ... more in your attitude. I have had a complaint.

JACK [*indignant*] About me? Who from?

JOHN William Randulph. You sat in the house while I examined his wife and he complains that you looked lewdly at his daughter Agness.

JACK Who says?

JOHN His daughter Agness.

JACK She'd say anything!

JOHN She did not say anything ... she said that you looked lewdly at her. Her sister is witness.

JACK They back one another up, don't they? They want the world to think that men look lewdly at them because it shows they've got something worth looking lewdly at!

JOHN What happened? Did you look at her?

JACK Yes ... I looked.

JOHN Then you looked lewdly ... because in my short experience of you, you've never looked at a woman in any other way.

JACK What should I do? Go about with my eyes shut?

JOHN To you it's a joke. To me as a medical man it's serious. How will women trust us to make examination of them ... how will parents trust us with their daughters? Leave the man in you well behind when you become the medical man. Dull your sense of female desirability by sharpening your sense of enquiry. In examining the most womanly of bodies you are simply there to detect the wormcast of disease. [*Pause.*] I'm due to write to your father soon.

[*Jack is instantly on his guard.*]

JACK But I hope I'll have the chance to put this matter right, doctor.

JOHN As long as you understand the reason . . .

JACK No, no. I see the point, doctor . . . I do.

JOHN I think your father hoped that an exact study like medicine would cool the heat a little.

JACK I'm foolish about women, doctor. It's a terrible weakness and it's all the worse because I believe I've been given an unfair burden to bear. I don't think any of the men I know suffers it like I do. I can go into a room where there's a young woman like Agness Randulph and no matter how I try to control it she seems in my mind to grow and grow until she fills the whole space and I'm gasping for breath in the corner! I see a short of shimmer . . . and I sweat . . . and the hairs on my body seem to bristle and raise up!

JOHN Perhaps we should make you up a prescription. Melissa officinalis . . . lemon balm . . . is good for anxiety disorders. I'll require you to apologise to the family.

[*Jack is relieved that it can be dealt with by a mere form of words.*]

JACK A man with no guts to apologise is no man at all!

JOHN I'm sure that's true. Do it this afternoon.

An Ideal Husband
Oscar Wilde

This society comedy was first performed in 1895 at the Haymarket Theatre, London.

The action centres around the moral dilemma of Sir Robert Chiltern, Under-Secretary for Foreign Affairs, who twenty years previously sold information on state documents in order to finance his political career, and is now being blackmailed by the unscrupulous Mrs Cheveley.

The opening scene of the third act is set in Lord Goring's library, where Phipps is arranging newspapers on the writing table. He is the Ideal Butler – 'a mask with a manner' – his main distinction being his impassivity. Lord Goring enters in evening dress wearing a buttonhole. He has a silk hat, Inverness cape, white gloves and carries a Louis Seize cane. Described by his friend, Sir Robert, as 'the idlest man in London' and by his father as 'a conceited young puppy', he is, however, extremely clever, but prefers to hide behind the façade of the 'flawless dandy'.

Published by A&C Black, London

Act Three

LORD GORING Got my second buttonhole for me, Phipps?

PHIPPS Yes, my lord.

[*Takes his hat, cane and cape, and presents new buttonhole on salver.*]

LORD GORING Rather distinguished thing, Phipps. I am the only person of the smallest importance in London at present who wears a buttonhole.

PHIPPS Yes, my lord. I have observed that.

LORD GORING [*taking out old buttonhole*] You see, Phipps, Fashion is what one wears oneself. What is unfashionable is what other people wear.

PHIPPS Yes, my lord.

LORD GORING Just as vulgarity is simply the conduct of other people.

PHIPPS Yes, my lord.

LORD GORING [*putting in new buttonhole*] And falsehoods the truths of other people.

PHIPPS Yes, my lord.

LORD GORING Other people are quite dreadful. The only possible society is oneself.

PHIPPS Yes, my lord.

LORD GORING To love oneself is the beginning of a life-long romance, Phipps.

PHIPPS Yes, my lord.

LORD GORING [*looking at himself in the glass*] Don't think I quite like this buttonhole, Phipps. Makes me look a little too old. Makes me almost in the prime of life, eh, Phipps?

PHIPPS I don't observe any alteration in your lordship's appearance.

LORD GORING You don't, Phipps?

PHIPPS No, my lord.

LORD GORING I am not quite sure. For the future a more trivial buttonhole, Phipps, on Thursday evenings.

PHIPPS I will speak to the florist, my lord. She has had a loss in her family lately, which perhaps accounts for the lack of triviality your lordship complains of in the buttonhole.

LORD GORING Extraordinary thing about the lower classes in England – they are always losing their relations.

PHIPPS Yes, my lord! They are extremely fortunate in that respect.

LORD GORING [*Turns round and looks at him. Phipps remains impassive.*]

Hum! Any letters, Phipps?

PHIPPS Three, my lord.

[*Hands letters on a salver.*]

LORD GORING [*takes letters*] Want my cab round in twenty minutes.

PHIPPS Yes, my lord.

[*Goes towards door.*]

LORD GORING [*holds up letter in pink envelope*] Ahem! Phipps, when did this letter arrive?

PHIPPS It was brought by hand just after your lordship went to the Club.

LORD GORING That will do.

JACK WORTHING
young

ALGERNON MONCRIEFF
young

The Importance of Being Earnest
Oscar Wilde

This comedy of manners was first performed at St James's Theatre, London in 1895.

At the beginning of the play Jack Worthing explains to his friend, Algernon, that he always assumes the name of a mythical younger brother, 'Ernest', when he is in town, in order to excuse his frequent absences from his country home. However, when his beloved Gwendolen agrees to marry him, she declares that she chiefly loves him because his name is 'Ernest'. Meanwhile, Jack's young ward, Cecily, who has always been fascinated by his mythical younger brother, meets Algernon, who has called himself 'Ernest' in order to gain admittance to Jack's country home. They fall in love at first sight and she also declares that she could only love an 'Ernest'.

In this scene Jack and Algernon have decided simultaneously that the only way out of their problem is to have themselves christened.

Published by A&C Black, London

Act Two

JACK How you can sit there, calmly eating muffins when we are in this horrible trouble, I can't make out. You seem to me to be perfectly heartless.

ALGERNON Well, I can't eat muffins in an agitated manner. The butter would probably get on my cuffs. One should always eat muffins quite calmly. It is the only way to eat them.

JACK I say it's perfectly heartless your eating muffins at all, under the circumstances.

ALGERNON When I am in trouble, eating is the only thing that consoles me. Indeed, when I am in really great trouble, as anyone who knows me intimately will tell you, I refuse everything except food and drink. At the present moment I am eating muffins because I am unhappy. Besides, I am particularly fond of muffins. [*Rising.*]

JACK [*rising*] Well, that is no reason why you should eat them all in that greedy way. [*Takes muffins from Algernon.*]

ALGERNON [*offering tea-cake*] I wish you would have tea-cake instead. I don't like tea-cake.

JACK Good heavens! I suppose a man may eat his own muffins in his own garden.

ALGERNON But you have just said it was perfectly heartless to eat muffins.

JACK I said it was perfectly heartless of you, under the circumstances. That is a very different thing.

ALGERNON That may be, but the muffins are the same. [*He seizes the muffin-dish from Jack.*]

JACK Algy, I wish to goodness you would go.

ALGERNON You can't possibly ask me to go without having some dinner. It's absurd. I never go without my dinner. No one ever does, except vegetarians and people like that. Besides I have just made arrangements with Dr Chasuble to be christened at a quarter to six under the name of Ernest.

JACK My dear fellow, the sooner you give up that nonsense the better. I made arrangements this morning with Dr Chasuble to be christened myself at 5.30, and I naturally will take the name of Ernest. Gwendolen would wish it. We can't both be christened Ernest. It's absurd. Besides, I have a perfect right to be christened if I like. There is no evidence at all that I ever have been christened by anybody. I should think it extremely probable I never was, and so does Dr Chasuble. It is entirely different in your case. You have been christened already.

ALGERNON Yes, but I have not been christened for years.

JACK Yes, but you have been christened. That is the important thing.

ALGERNON Quite so. So I know my constitution can stand it. If you are not quite sure about your ever having been christened, I must say I think it rather dangerous your venturing on it now. It might make you very unwell. You can hardly have forgotten that someone very closely connected with you was very nearly carried off this week in Paris by a severe chill.

JACK Yes, but you said yourself that a severe chill was not hereditary.

ALGERNON It usen't to be, I know – but I daresay it is now. Science is always making wonderful improvements in things.

JACK [*picking up the muffin-dish*] Oh, that is nonsense; you are always talking nonsense.

ALGERNON Jack, you are at the muffins again! I wish you wouldn't. There are only two left. [*Takes them.*] I told you I was particularly fond of muffins.

JACK But I hate tea-cake.

ALGERNON Why on earth then do you allow tea-cake to be served up for your guests? What ideas you have of hospitality!

JACK Algernon! I have already told you to go. I don't want you here. Why don't you go!

ALGERNON I haven't quite finished my tea yet! and there is still one muffin left.

[*Jack groans, and sinks into a chair. Algernon still continues eating.*]

UPSIDE DOWN   UPRIGHT
teens   teens
Liverpool   Liverpool

On the Ledge
Alan Bleasdale

First performed at the Nottingham Playhouse in 1993 and later at the Lyttleton Theatre in London.

The action takes place mainly on the roof and ledges of a multi-storey block of flats. In this opening scene, two Liverpool lads in their teens are on the flat roof. One is being held upside down over the railings by the other lad. They are referred to throughout the play as Upside Down and Upright. Upside Down has a pot of paint in one hand and a paint brush in the other. He is completing the legend 'ANACHRY RULES' (sic) whilst Upright, holding him not too tightly by the ankles, describes his visit to London.

Published by Faber & Faber, London

Act One

UPSIDE DOWN ... London, hey?

UPRIGHT [*sourly*] Yeah, London.

UPSIDE DOWN I wondered where you'd been.

UPRIGHT I'm not goin' again. The bastards hate us.

UPSIDE DOWN But what's it really like down South?

UPRIGHT I don't know. I wasn't there long enough.

UPSIDE DOWN Y've been gone a year. At least.

UPRIGHT But I was only down there six months ... [*very thoughtfully*] ... before the bastards got me ... bastard Cockney police ... bastard Cockney courtroom ... bastard Cockney jury ... bastard Cockney barristers ... bastard Cockney judge—

UPSIDE DOWN The judge was a Cockney?

UPRIGHT [*oblivious*] – Bastard Cockney detention centre – bastard Cockney police escort up the bastard Cockney M1 ... bastard nine months in Wakefield gaol ... no time off for good behaviour because I wouldn't bastard well behave ... bastard Edwina Currie.

UPSIDE DOWN I know . . . What? Edwina Currie?

UPRIGHT It's all her fault, her and that bastard Peter Bastard Sissons and all the other bastards on his bastard *Question Time* . . . because of them, the bastard I was robbin' turned his bastard telly off.

UPSIDE DOWN D'you blame him?

UPRIGHT Came in the bastard back-kitchen, didn't he, the Cockney bastard, and bastard well caught me . . . bastard black eye . . . bastard broken nose, broken bones, bastard boot in the balls . . . bastard frostbite—

UPSIDE DOWN Frostbite?

UPRIGHT I'm comin' to that . . . bastard hospital . . . bastard intensive care.

UPSIDE DOWN Was he a big bastard?

UPRIGHT Bastard body builder . . . If I'd been thinking straight, if I'd have been a proper robber, I'd have realized – I'd just robbed his fuckin' Bullworker . . .

UPSIDE DOWN Typical.

[*Upright looks down. Contemplates. Grins.*]

UPRIGHT . . . Still get like, y'know, side effects.

UPSIDE DOWN Oh yeah? Like what?

UPRIGHT Oh nothin', just me wrists sometimes give way on me. Without warnin'.

[*He shakes Upside Down by the ankles, and ruins the 'R' in 'RULES'.*]

UPSIDE DOWN Y'bastard!

UPRIGHT I know. Still, it had a sort of happy ending . . . I might have got nine months but that bastard body builder got three and a half years for attempted murder. Serves him fuckin' well right. I'm tellin' y', he was fuckin' deranged; it's no fun bein' locked in a fuckin' big chest freezer, y'know . . . I'll never forget lyin' there on the floor with his foot on me throat while he's emptyin' it out, screamin', 'Die, y'Scouse bastard!', fuckin' frozen sprouts and tubs of ice-cream bouncin' all around me . . . and then fuck off, into his freezer . . . the police had to wait until I was defrosted before they could interview me . . . still be there now if his wife hadn't come home and told him the cost of letting frozen sirloin steak go to waste.

UPSIDE DOWN [*Cockney*] 'Got anything in the freezer, girl?'

UPRIGHT [*Cockney*] 'Only that fuckin' thief you caught last year, Eric.'

45

UPSIDE DOWN [*Cockney*] 'Put him in the microwave, let's have some Scouse.'

[*They both laugh. Upside Down is finishing off the 'S' in 'RULES'.*]

UPRIGHT ... Life's a bastard, all right. That's what life is.

UPSIDE DOWN It's finished now.

[*Upside Down puts the paint brush in the pot.*]

UPRIGHT Don't depress me, Billy. Not at my age. I'm depressed enough. Life might be a bastard but don't tell me it's finished.

UPSIDE DOWN No—

UPRIGHT That's why I went down South.

[*Upright becomes impassioned. Upside Down gets shaken about.*]

I wasn't goin' down there to thieve. Was I fuck. I was just goin' down there to you know like *achieve* – ended up in Hammersmith. Under the bastard bridge.

UPSIDE DOWN Listen—

UPRIGHT Open y'mouth down there – y'fuckin' accent stands up in court an' pleads guilty on y'behalf. No wonder the bastard Cockneys call it y'North an' South. Pretended to be from Scotland.

UPSIDE DOWN *Jimmy, f'fuck's sake, will y'listen to me!*

[*Upright lets go of Upside Down with one hand and points an admonishing finger at him.*]

UPRIGHT Don't interrupt. It's bad manners to interrupt.

[*Upside Down dangles one leg free until Upright, his dignity and position firmly established, takes hold of both ankles again.*]

Anyway, I pretended I was from Glasgow once, 'cos it was the only other accent I could do – 'Och aye, the fuckin' noo, Jimmy.'

UPSIDE DOWN *Jimmy!*

UPRIGHT I should have known – the bastards don't like the Jocks neither.

UPSIDE DOWN No no, listen to me, it's me paintin', that's what's finished. An' I'm goin' all dizzy! Get me up will y'!

D'ARCY TUCK   FREDDY MALONE
young   young

Plunder

Ben Travers

This classic farce was first performed at the Aldwych Theatre, London in 1928.

Joan Hewlett returns from New Zealand with her fiancé, D'Arcy Tuck, expecting to claim the estate left to her by her grandfather, only to find that his unscrupulous housekeeper married the old man just before his death and has taken over the house and contents, including a large amount of jewellery. The action revolves around the attempt of D'Arcy Tuck and his old schoolfriend, Freddy Malone, turned professional thief, to stage the perfect robbery and hand over to Joan the jewellery which should have been part of her inheritance.

In this scene, Freddy explains to D'Arcy how he and his sister, Prudence, had already intended to steal Mrs Hewlett's jewels, but is now willing to cut him in on half of the proceeds.

Published in *Five Plays*, Ben Travers, by W.H. Allen, London

Act One

D'ARCY I'm gong to know the truth. What are you doing here with these people?

FREDDY Well, listen. You're out to do that old woman down. Aren't you?

D'ARCY Well, haven't you been listening? Of course I am.

FREDDY So am I, you fool.

D'ARCY *You* are? In what way?

FREDDY I can see I shall have to take a hell of a risk with you. I'm going to let you into something.

D'ARCY Let me into something?

FREDDY Hold on. We'll have this in writing. [*Sits at table and prepares to write.*]

D'ARCY Why? Who are you going to write to?

FREDDY I'll put it in your own words. 'We agree to get level with Mrs Hewlett by any means, fair or foul. Freddy Malone.' [*Handing pen to D'Arcy.*] Go on. 'D'Arcy Tuck.' You sign it too.

D'ARCY Good Lord! But even so, why write it? I don't like writing things. It's a bit of a risk.

FREDDY It's nothing to the risk I'm taking with you. Go on.

D'ARCY [*puzzled, hesitating*] All right. Still – I – don't think I'm very keen on – on this pen. [*Signs.*] There you are. [*About to blot it.*]

FREDDY [*quickly*] Don't blot it.
[*Freddy pockets paper.*]

D'ARCY But why should *you* take it?

FREDDY To stop your silly tongue.
[*Crosses to window, closes it, comes back.*]
I've got to take a big chance with you. Either that or lose a very good thing.

D'ARCY What thing?

FREDDY What I'm going to tell you will be a bit of a shock. You'll find it difficult to believe. D'you remember at school we had an oath? There was an old stinks master with a beard – Allah we called him.

D'ARCY Yes. We used to swear by the beard of Allah.

FREDDY Yes, and it held. You and I have been all over the world since then and broken every commandment in turn. But did you ever break that oath – by the beard of Allah?

D'ARCY No. No one ever broke that. It was sacred.

FREDDY Right. You're going to swear it now.

D'ARCY Swear what?

FREDDY That what I'm about to tell you you'll never repeat.

D'ARCY Good Lord! Is it as bad as that?

FREDDY It's vital. Come on. Asleep or awake – sober or tight – you'll never tell a soul. Swear that.

D'ARCY I swear by the beard of Allah.

FREDDY Sit down.
[*D'Arcy sits. Freddy sits on his right.*]
Now I'll tell you what I'm here for.

D'ARCY Well? What are you here for?

FREDDY Plunder.

D'ARCY Plunder? What do you mean?

FREDDY That's what I do. That's how I live. That's my profession.

D'ARCY Do you mean you're a cr . . .

[*Freddy gestures with his hand to stop him.*]

FREDDY Only one other man knows it and he's a foreigner in Marseilles. And one woman. My accomplice. Passes as my sister.

D'ARCY She's *not* your sister. Why do you say she is?

FREDDY Purely for business purposes.

D'ARCY But you! Your friends! The people you know!

FREDDY Yes, rather. All the topnotchers. I'm Freddy to them all, aren't I? Quite a lad. Yachtsman – big game shot, anything you like. Oh yes – I do it on very high-class lines.

D'ARCY But what is it – that you do?

FREDDY Steal.

D'ARCY What?

FREDDY Steal.

D'ARCY Steal? But, good Lord, man, why?

FREDDY I like it.

D'ARCY You like it?

FREDDY I love it.

D'ARCY I don't believe it. [*Feels for his watch-chain – he can't find it for a second and gets a shock.*] What! Wait a minute! [*Finds it.*] No, I don't believe you.

FREDDY Don't worry. I'm not that sort of thief.

D'ARCY What do you thieve?

FREDDY Jewels, for choice, from big houses.

D'ARCY What? A house-lifter!

FREDDY That's why I'm here. Hers are worth a packet.

D'ARCY You're going to take them?

FREDDY I am. All of them. She hasn't got them all here. Some are in the bank.

D'ARCY You're not going to break into the bank?

FREDDY No. She's coming to stay at my house. She'll have them all with her then. I've seen to that.

D'ARCY But if you were caught?

FREDDY I'm not. I make that one of my strictest rules.

D'ARCY This all is a lie. Society crooks are only in books.
    [*Freddy rings.*]

FREDDY Oh, very well.

D'ARCY What are you doing?

FREDDY If there's time, I'll prove it to you.

D'ARCY How long – do you pretend – you've been like this?

FREDDY Always. D'you remember that half-mile challenge cup that got lifted at school? That was me.

D'ARCY Good Lord! And I *won* it.

FREDDY One of my earliest recollections is my father catching me cheating at cards. He caught me taking an ace from my shirt.

D'ARCY Good Lord! Then he ought to have lifted your shirt and flogged it.

FREDDY He did. And after the flogging he showed me how to pull out the ace without being caught.

D'ARCY Appalling! [*Pause.*] How do you pull out the ace?

FREDDY I'd show you, only I don't happen to have an ace in my shirt at the moment . . .

D'ARCY Tell me this. Where did you run across this old woman?

FREDDY A few days ago at Monte Carlo. She'd come in for this money and she was flashing the jewels all over her stomach.

D'ARCY [*bitterly*] Our money – Joan's and mine – and our jewels.

FREDDY Yes, old boy, but her stomach. I couldn't take them then. I'd just pulled off another job and the police were on a false scent so I let them stay there.

D'ARCY Oh, so that's why you're friends with them? That's why your sister's encouraging this – this growth?

FREDDY That's it. And they're coming to stay with us on the tenth. And so's the jewellery.

Sleuth

Anthony Shaffer

First performed at The Music Box, New York in 1970 and later at St Martin's Theatre, London.

The action takes place in an English country house owned by middle-aged mystery writer, Andrew Wyke – a man who enjoys playing games, particularly cruel or dangerous ones. While his wife is away, he invites her lover, Milo Tindle, over for drinks. Gradually Milo finds himself drawn into playing a game with tragic consequences. At the end of the first act Andrew has shot Milo, and we see him lying apparently dead at the foot of the stairs.

In this scene, Inspector Doppler of the Wiltshire constabulary is in the middle of questioning Andrew about the disappearance of Milo Tindle.

Published by Samuel French Inc., New York

Act Two

ANDREW It's all so difficult ...

DOPPLER On the contrary, sir, I think it's all very simple. I think you started this exactly as you say you did, as a game, in order to play a diabolical trick on Mr Tindle, but that it went wrong. Your third shot was not a blank as you had supposed, but was in fact a live bullet which killed Mr Tindle stone dead, spattering his blood on the bannister in the process. When you realized what you'd done you panicked and buried him in the garden. It was silly of you not to wash the blood properly off the bannister and burn his clothes though.

ANDREW I've told you Tindle left here alive.

DOPPLER I don't believe it.

ANDREW I didn't murder him.

DOPPLER I accept that. As I said, I think it happened by accident. We'll be quite content with a charge of manslaughter.

ANDREW I did not kill him! He left here alive.

DOPPLER If you will pardon a flippancy, sir, you had better tell that to the judge.

ANDREW Look. There's one way of settling this. If you think Tindle is in the garden, go and dig him up.

DOPPLER We don't need to find him, sir. Recent decisions have relieved the prosecution of producing the corpus delicti. If Mr Tindle is not under the newly turned earth, it will merely indicate that in your panic you first thought of putting him there, then changed your mind and buried him somewhere else.

ANDREW Where?

DOPPLER Does it matter? Spook Spinney! Flasher's Heath! It's all the same to us. He'll turn up sooner or later – discovered by some adulterous salesman, or over-sexed boy scout. And if he doesn't, it scarcely matters, there's so much circumstantial evidence against you. Come along, it's time to go.

ANDREW Go! What do you mean go? I'm not going anywhere!

DOPPLER I'm afraid I must insist, sir! There's a police car outside.

ANDREW You can have twenty police cars out there. I'm not going.

DOPPLER Now let's have no trouble, sir. Please don't make it difficult.

ANDREW [*wildly*] I must see a lawyer. It's my right.

DOPPLER We can make a call from the station, sir. We wouldn't want to do anything unconstitutional. Come on, sir. At the most you'll only get seven years!

ANDREW [*horrified*] Seven years!

DOPPLER Seven years to regret playing silly games that go wrong.

ANDREW [*bitterly*] It didn't go wrong. It went absolutely right. You've trapped me somehow.

DOPPLER Yes, sir. You see, we real life detectives aren't as stupid as we are sometimes portrayed by writers like yourself. We may not have our deer-stalker hats, our pipes, or our orchid houses, but we tend to be reasonably effective for all that.

ANDREW Who the hell are you?

DOPPLER Detective Inspector Doppler, sir, spelt as in C. Doppler 1803–1853 whose principle it was that when the source of any wave movement is approached, the frequency appears greater than it would to an observer moving away. It is also not unconnected with the German word Dopple meaning double – hence

Doppleganger or double in age. And of course, for those whose minds run to these things, it is virtually an anagram of the word Plodder. Inspector Plodder becomes Inspector Doppler, if you see what I mean, sir! [*Milo removes his disguise.*]

ANDREW [*a shriek*] Milo!

MILO [*normal voice*] The same.

ANDREW You shit!

MILO Just so.

ANDREW You platinum-plated, copper-bottomed, dyed in the wool, all-time, knock-down, dragout, champion bastard Milo!

MILO Thanks.

ANDREW You weasel! You cozening coypu! You mendacious bollock of Satan.

MILO Obliged.

ANDREW Milo! You triple-dealing turd!

MILO In your debt.

ANDREW Mind you, I'm not saying it wasn't well done. It was absolutely brilliant.

MILO Thank you.

ANDREW Have a drink, my dear fellow.

MILO Let me wash first. I'm covered in make-up and spirit gum.

ANDREW Just down the corridor there on your right. Cheers!

MILO Good health.

MICHAEL	EDWARD
young/middle-aged	mid-30s
English	Northern Irish

Someone Who'll Watch Over Me
Frank McGuinness

First performed at Hampstead Theatre, London in 1992.

An Englishman, an Irishman and an American are locked up together in a cell in the Middle East. In this scene the American has been taken out and possibly executed. Michael, who was teaching English at the University when he was captured, is eating his meal from a bowl. Edward, a journalist from Northern Ireland, has left his food untouched.

Published by Faber & Faber, London

Scene Six

MICHAEL This is good.

[*He eats more in silence.*]

It's chicken. The vegetables are fresh as well. A bit overcooked for me. Undercooked for you, I'd say. But it's good.

[*Silence.*]

Aren't you going to eat? You must be hungry.

[*Silence.*]

You haven't eaten for three days. They're getting worried about you not eating.

[*Silence.*]

This not talking, this not eating, isn't going to help us. We are in a decidedly perilous position, to put it mildly. You might say, put nothing mildly. But we can't push them too far. Push them as far as we can push them, is that it? Then they are liable to turn very nasty indeed. They are in quite a state as it stands. They know what they have done. At the moment they are hovering between apology and arrogance. Trying very hard as I am to take some rational – some comfort out of this, I do feel they themselves did not wish to kill Adam—

He is dead. I have evidence of that, as have you. My evidence
is that one of them actually wept—
[*Silence.*]
That's an act he was putting on to mock us, is that what you
think? One of them wept when he came into this – this cell.
There is no point in believing that. That's a lie? A complete
lie? Don't fall for that, yes? They have him in hiding some-
where else? Your main worry is that he may be on his own.
He did manage on his own when they first got him. He will
manage now. But you are not eating until he is brought back
here to us? He is not dead? You firmly believe that. Nothing
I can say will convince you otherwise? Do I understand you?
[*Silence.*]
EDWARD They would not kill him.
MICHAEL What would he have done to stop them?
[*Silence.*]
Adam is dead, Edward.
EDWARD You want him dead. You feel safer with him dead. One
of us down, and no more to go. With him dead there'll be a
big outcry and we will be saved. Isn't that it? Well, listen, get
that out of your head, for if they've put him down, they can
put us down as well. Dogs together, to be shot. Take no conso-
lation from imagining him dead. It won't save you. It won't
save me.
MICHAEL No, it won't save you. You hope it might save you,
but you're perfectly correct, his death won't save you. You
condemn yourself out of your own mouth. It isn't me who
wants him dead. It's you, isn't it?
[*Silence.*]
I don't blame you for thinking that. You want to give his death
some – some sense of sacrifice. You are in grief, in mourning.
And you are mad with grief.
EDWARD He is not—
MICHAEL [*roars*] Dead, he is, and you know it.
EDWARD You know nothing.
MICHAEL I know about grief. About mourning. How it can
destroy you. I know.
[*Silence.*]
You know he's dead, don't you?
[*Silence.*]
Say it, he is dead.
[*Silence.*]

EDWARD He died. I needed him. Jesus, I needed him.
[*Silence.*]
How could he leave me? How could he do this? Without him, how will I get through this?
MICHAEL Bury him.
[*Silence.*]
Remember him.
[*Silence.*]
What was he like?
EDWARD He was gentle. He was kind. He could be cruel, when he was afraid, and while he was often afraid, as we all are afraid, he was not often cruel. He was brave, he could protect himself, and me, and you. He was beautiful to look at. I watched him as he slept one night I couldn't sleep. He moved that night through his sleep like a man not dreaming of what life had in store for him. He was innocent. Kind, gentle. Friend. I believe it goes without saying, love, so I never said. He is dead. Bury him. Perpetual light shine upon him. May his soul rest in peace. Amen.
[*Silence.*]
MICHAEL Love bade me welcome: yet my soul drew back,
Guiltie of dust and sinne.
But quick-ey'd Love, observing me grow slack
From my first entrance in,
Drew nearer to me, sweetly questioning,
If I lack'd anything.

A guest, I answer'd, worthy to be here:
Love said, You shall be he.
I the unkinde, ungratefull? Ah my deare,
I cannot look on thee.
Love took my hand, and smiling did reply,
Who made the eyes but I?

Truth Lord, but I have marr'd them: Let my shame
Go where it doth deserve.
And know you not, sayes Love, who bore the blame?
My deare, then I will serve.
You must sit down, sayes Love, and taste my meat:
So I did sit and eat.
[*Silence.*]
EDWARD I'm hungry.
MICHAEL Then eat.

EDWARD Dear friend.
  [*Edward eats.*]
  He's dead.
MICHAEL We are not.

REG WELSH   ARTHUR HOYLE
middle-aged   middle-aged
Yorkshire   Yorkshire

Up 'n' Under
John Godber

First performed by the Hull Truck Company in 1984 and transferred to the Fortune Theatre, London in 1985. The play is
dedicated to the Rugby League fans of Hull.

At the opening of the play, Frank Rowley, local butcher and
member of the notoriously unsuccessful Wheatsheaf Arms
rugby team, addresses the audience and introduces two old
rivals, Reg Welsh, manager of the Cobblers – 'unbeaten gods
of amateur rugby sevens' – and Arthur Hoyle, hero of the
story and soon to become manager of the Wheatsheaf side.

In this scene Arthur, who is 'apt to make daft bets', challenges the might of the Cobblers. And Reg, who is a gambling
man, takes up the challenge.

Published in *Five Plays*, John Godber, by Penguin Plays, London

Act One
REG Arthur ...
ARTHUR Reg ...
REG How are you, sunshine?
ARTHUR Not bad ...
REG How's the wife?
ARTHUR Still living in the same house.
REG Like that, is it, Arthur?
ARTHUR You know Doreen, Reg, she'd argue with fog.
REG Takes after you, Arthur.
ARTHUR Dunno.
REG No.
ARTHUR No, I've changed, Reg ... I was a hothead, you know
    that as well as anybody ... I've cooled down.
REG Good to hear that, Arth.
ARTHUR Well, old age and poverty helps, doesn't it?

REG Dunno about the poverty.

ARTHUR No, right.

REG You did some daft things in your day, Arthur lad.

ARTHUR I know.

REG Can you remember when you poked the linesman in the eye at Warrington?

ARTHUR I can.

REG And when you head-butted the referee at St Helens?

ARTHUR Yeah.

REG Eh, and when you burnt down the goal posts at 'Unslett?

ARTHUR Oh, for disagreeing with that offside decision.

REG Didn't see that one, read about it in the paper.

ARTHUR Good times, Reg.

REG Yes.

ARTHUR Good times.

REG I must say, Arthur ... it's good to see you settled.

ARTHUR Oh, yeah ...

REG The way you were going I never thought you'd make thirty.

ARTHUR No.

REG You could still have been playing.

ARTHUR If it hadn't been for you, Reg.

REG Now don't be like that, Arth.

ARTHUR But it's true, you were on the board that got me banned, you know that as much as anybody.

REG Let's not get into all that ...

ARTHUR You brought it up.

REG No matter what I say to you I'll not convince you that it wasn't only me who pushed to have you banned ... no matter what I say ...

ARTHUR That's the way I saw it, anyway ...

[*A beat.*]

REG Cigar?

ARTHUR Don't smoke.

REG Still fit?

ARTHUR Still trying.

REG Good to hear it.

ARTHUR We can't all live a life of leisure, can we, Reg?

REG But I've worked for it, Arthur sunshine ... worked for it ... making money is all about having money, investing money.

ARTHUR Yeah ...

REG You must have a bob or two?

ARTHUR I've got a bob or two.

REG I thought so.

ARTHUR And that's all I've got.

REG What do you think to my lads this year?

ARTHUR All right.

REG Come on, Arthur, ... they're more than all right, they're magnificent ... The Magnificent Seven, that's what I call them.

ARTHUR They've got their problems, Reg.

REG What do you mean?

ARTHUR They're good on the ball ...

REG Yeah ...

ARTHUR Bad in defence.

REG Give over ... their defence is clam-tight.

ARTHUR No, is it, heck.

REG It is.

ARTHUR Well, you take it from me.

REG The Cobblers'll beat any side you want to name.

ARTHUR They're not that good, Reg ... listen to me, I'm telling you.

REG I thought you might have learnt some sense as times go on ... pity you haven't ... same old Arthur.

ARTHUR Same old Reg ... full of shit.

REG Oh, you're not worth talking to.

ARTHUR The truth hurts.

REG You make me laugh ... a feller with half an eye could see how good they are.

ARTHUR In that case I must be going blind.

REG Look at that ... free and economic distribution ... fast hands ... unbeatable ... completely unbeatable.

ARTHUR No.

REG They are.

ARTHUR Reg, they're not.

REG I'm not arguing with you ... you know I'm right.

ARTHUR I could train a team to beat 'em.

REG Talk sense.

ARTHUR I am talking sense.

REG Doesn't sound like much sense to me.

ARTHUR I could get a team together to beat the Cobblers.

REG Have you had some beer?

ARTHUR No.

REG Can you hear what you're saying?

ARTHUR I know what I'm saying and I mean it ... I've thought it for years.

REG Arthur, you're talking out of your arsehole.

ARTHUR Steady.

REG You are talking utter crap and you know it.

ARTHUR No, I'm not. I could get a team to beat 'em.

REG Don't be such a pillock.

ARTHUR I said, steady with the language, Reg.

REG Well, you're talking such rubbish, man.

ARTHUR I'm not talking rubbish, I'm talking facts ... there's a way to beat these, no problem.

REG There's no way you're gonna get an amateur club to beat these, no way.

ARTHUR Rubbish.

REG No way.

ARTHUR Rubbish.

REG No way, Arthur ...

ARTHUR I could do it ... I could train any team in the North to beat these.

REG OK then, put your money where your mouth is.

ARTHUR Eh ... ?

REG Put your money where your mouth is.

ARTHUR Ar ... dunno ...

REG See what I mean? You're the one who's full of shit.

ARTHUR All right, then, I bet you ...

REG That you can train a given team to beat my lads?

ARTHUR Yeah, I bet you, Reg.

REG How much? Four grand ... five thousand ... Ten thousand, Arthur? Let's make it a decent bet, shall we?

ARTHUR I bet my mortgage ...

REG What about Doreen?

ARTHUR I bet my house ...

REG Keep it sensible.

ARTHUR I bet my house that I can get a team to beat them set of nancy poofters, Reg Welsh ... that's the bet, shake on it.

REG You'll lose ...

ARTHUR We'll see ...

REG I mean it.

ARTHUR Any team in the North, come on, name a club side ... I'll train 'em.

REG We'll meet in the next sevens.

ARTHUR When is it?

REG Five weeks' time.

ARTHUR That's great ... name my name.

REG No turning back . . .

ARTHUR You've got my word.

REG It's a bet?

ARTHUR Come on, name the team I've got to train.

REG I'll make arrangements for us to meet in the draw.

ARTHUR I'll leave the dirty work to you.

REG I'll pull a few influential strings.

ARTHUR What's the team, Reg?

REG I name the Wheatsheaf from near Hull.

ARTHUR Nice one . . . now name a team.

REG I name the Wheatsheaf, Arthur.

ARTHUR The Wheatsheaf Arms?

REG That's the one.

ARTHUR You're joking.

REG The bet's on.

ARTHUR Bloody hell . . .

REG Five weeks then, Arthur . . . I look forward to the game . . .

DOG   CUDDY
any age   young

The Witch of Edmonton
William Rowley, Thomas Dekker and John Ford

A tragi-comedy written in 1621 and performed at The Cockpit
in Drury Lane.

Old Mother Sawyer – the witch – has sold her soul to the
Devil, who appeared to her in the shape of a black dog, so
that she might be revenged on all those that harmed her. The
dog, known as Tommy, is befriended early in the play by
Cuddy Banks, a simple village lad.

Now the witch is about to be hanged and Cuddy meets his
friend for the last time – in the shape of a white dog.

Published by A&C Black, London in 1998

Act Five, Scene One

CUDDY I would fain meet with mine ningle once more: he has
had a claw amongst 'em: my rival that loved my wench is like
to be hanged like an innocent. A kind cur where he takes, but
where he takes not, a dogged rascal; I know the villain loves
me. No, – [*The Dog barks.*] No! art thou there? [*Seeing the
Dog*] that's Tom's voice, but 'tis not he; this is a dog of another
hair, this. Bark, and not speak to me? not Tom then; there's
as much difference betwixt Tom and this as betwixt white and
black.

DOG Hast thou forgot me?

CUDDY That's Tom again.—Prithee, ningle, speak: is thy name
Tom?

DOG Whilst I served my old Dame Sawyer 'twas; I'm gone from
her now.

CUDDY Gone? Away with the witch, then, too! she'll never thrive
if thou leavest her; she knows no more how to kill a cow, or
a horse, or a sow, without thee, than she does to kill a goose.

DOG No, she has done killing now, but must be kill'd for what
she has done; she's shortly to be hanged.

CUDDY Is she? in my conscience, if she be, 'tis thou hast brought
  her to the gallows, Tom.

DOG Right. I served her to that purpose; 'twas part of my wages.

CUDDY This was no honest servant's part, by your leave, Tom.
  This remember, I pray you, between you and I; I entertained
  you ever as a dog, not as a devil.

DOG True; And so I used thee doggedly, not devilishly;
  I have deluded thee for sport to laugh at:
  The wench thou seek'st after thou never spak'st with,
  But a spirit in her form, habit, and likeness. Ha, ha!

CUDDY I do not, then, wonder at the change of your garments,
  if you can enter into shapes of women too.

DOG Any shape, to blind such silly eyes as thine; but chiefly those
  coarse creatures, dog, or cat, hare, ferret, frog, toad.

CUDDY Louse or flea?

DOG Any poor vermin.

CUDDY It seems you devils have poor, thin souls, that you can
  bestow yourselves in such small bodies. But pray you, Tom,
  one question at parting; – I think I shall never see you more;
  – where do you borrow those bodies that are none of your
  own? – the garment-shape you may hire at broker's.

DOG Why would'st thou know that fool? it avails thee not.

CUDDY Only for my mind's sake, Tom, and to tell some of my
  friends.

DOG I'll thus much tell thee: Thou never art so distant
  From an evil spirit but that thy oaths,
  Curses, and blasphemies pull him to thine elbow;
  Thou never tell'st a lie but that a devil
  Is within hearing it; thy evil purposes
  Are ever haunted; but when they come to act, –
  As thy tongue slandering, bearing false witness,
  Thy hand stabbing, stealing, cozening, cheating, –
  He's then within thee: thou play'st, he bets upon thy part.
  Although thou lose, yet he will gain by thee.

CUDDY Ay? then he comes in the shape of a rook?

DOG The old cadaver of some self-strangled wretch
  We sometimes borrow, and appear human;
  The carcass of some disease-slain strumpet
  We varnish fresh, and wear as her first beauty.
  Did'st never hear? if not, it has been done;
  An hot, luxurious lecher in his twines,
  When he has thought to clip his dalliance,

There has provided been for his embrace
A fine hot flaming devil in her place.

CUDDY Yes, I am partly a witness to this; but I never could embrace her; I thank thee for that, Tom. Well, again I thank thee, Tom, for all this counsel; without a fee too! there's few lawyers of thy mind now. Certainly, Tom, I begin to pity thee.

DOG Pity me! For what?

CUDDY Were it not possible for thee to become an honest dog yet? – 'Tis a base life that you lead, Tom, to serve witches, to kill innocent children, to kill harmless cattle, to stroy corn and fruit, etc.: 'twere better yet to be a butcher and kill for yourself.

DOG Why? These are all my delights, my pleasures, fool.

CUDDY Or, Tom, if you could give your mind to ducking, – I know you can swim, fetch, and carry, – some shopkeeper in London would take great delight in you, and be a tender master over you: or if you have a mind to the game either at bull or bear, I think I could prefer you to Moll Cutpurse.

DOG Ha, ha! I should kill all the game, – bulls, bears, dogs and all; not a cub to be left.

CUDDY You could do, Tom; but you must play fair; you should be staved-off else. Or if your stomach did better like to serve in some nobleman's, knight's, or gentleman's kitchen, if you could brook the wheel and turn the spit – your labour could not be much – when they have roast meat, that's but once or twice in the week at most: here you might lick your own toes very well. Or if you could translate yourself into a lady's arming puppy, there you might lick sweet lips, and do many pretty offices; but to creep under an old witch's coats, and suck like a great puppy! fie upon't! – I have heard beastly things of you, Tom.

DOG Ha, ha! The worst thou heard'st of me, the better 'tis. Shall I serve thee, fool, at the selfsame rate?

CUDDY No, I'll see thee hanged; thou shalt be damned first. I know thy qualities too well, I'll give no suck to such whelps; therefore, henceforth I defy thee. Out, and avaunt!

DOG Nor will I serve for such a silly soul:
I am for greatness now ... hence, silly fool!
I scorn to prey on such an atom soul.

CUDDY Come out, come out, you cur! I will beat thee out of the bounds of Edmonton, and to-morrow we go in procession, and after thou shalt never come in again ... devil go with thee!
[*Exit, followed by the Dog barking.*]

EVE   SERPENT

Back to Methuselah
Bernard Shaw

First presented by the Theatre Guild at the Garrick Theatre, New York in 1922.

In his preface Shaw says that he has written this play as a contribution to the modern Bible.

In this first section – 'In the Beginning' – Adam and Eve are in the Garden of Eden and, curled around the branches of a great tree, is an immense Serpent. Adam has discovered a fawn lying with its neck broken. He calls to Eve and together they try to revive the creature. It is their first experience of death and they are very frightened. As Adam goes off to throw the fawn's body into the river, the Serpent becomes visible, glowing in wonderful new colours. She rears her head slowly and speaks seductively into Eve's ear.

Published in *Collected Plays with their Prefaces*, Bernard Shaw, by The Bodley Head, London

THE SERPENT Eve.

EVE [*startled*] Who is that?

THE SERPENT It is I. I have come to shew you my beautiful new hood. See [*she spreads a magnificent amethystine hood*]!

EVE [*admiring it*] Oh! But who taught you to speak?

THE SERPENT You and Adam. I have crept through the grass, and hidden, and listened to you.

EVE That was wonderfully clever of you.

THE SERPENT I am the most subtle of all the creatures of the field.

EVE Your hood is most lovely. [*She strokes it and pets the serpent.*] Pretty thing! Do you love your godmother Eve?

THE SERPENT I adore her. [*She licks Eve's neck with her double tongue.*]

EVE [*petting her*] Eve's wonderful darling snake. Eve will never be lonely now that her snake can talk to her.

THE SERPENT I can talk of many things. I am very wise. It was I who whispered the word to you that you did not know. Dead. Death. Die.

EVE [*shuddering*] Why do you remind me of it? I forgot it when I saw your beautiful hood. You must not remind me of unhappy things.

THE SERPENT Death is not an unhappy thing when you have learnt how to conquer it.

EVE How can I conquer it?

THE SERPENT By another thing, called birth.

EVE What? [*trying to pronounce it*] B-birth?

THE SERPENT Yes, birth.

EVE What is birth?

THE SERPENT The serpent never dies. Some day you shall see me come out of this beautiful skin, a new snake with a new and lovelier skin. That is birth.

EVE I have seen that. It is wonderful.

THE SERPENT If I can do that, what can I not do? I tell you I am very subtle. When you and Adam talk, I hear you say 'Why?' Always 'Why?' You see things; and you say 'Why?' But I dream things that never were; and I say 'Why not?' I made the word dead to describe my old skin that I cast when I am renewed. I call that renewal being born.

EVE Born is a beautiful word.

THE SERPENT Why not be born again and again as I am, new and beautiful every time?

EVE I! It does not happen: that is why.

THE SERPENT That is how; but it is not why. Why not?

EVE But I should not like it. It would be nice to be new again; but my old skin would lie on the ground looking just like me; and Adam would see it shrivel up and—

THE SERPENT No. He need not. There is a second birth.

EVE A second birth?

THE SERPENT Listen. I will tell you a great secret. I am very subtle; and I have thought and thought and thought. And I am very wilful, and must have what I want; and I have willed and willed and willed. And I have eaten strange things: stones and apples that you are afraid to eat.

EVE You dared!

THE SERPENT I dared everything. And at last I found a way of gathering together a part of the life in my body—

EVE What is the life?

THE SERPENT That which makes the difference between the dead fawn and the live one.

EVE What a beautiful word! And what a wonderful thing! Life is the loveliest of all the new words.

THE SERPENT Yes: it was by meditating on Life that I gained the power to do miracles.

EVE Miracles? Another new word.

THE SERPENT A miracle is an impossible thing that is nevertheless possible. Something that never could happen, and yet does happen.

EVE Tell me some miracle that you have done.

THE SERPENT I gathered a part of the life in my body, and shut it into a tiny white case made of the stones I had eaten.

EVE And what good was that?

THE SERPENT I shewed the little case to the sun, and left it in its warmth. And it burst; and a little snake came out; and it became bigger and bigger from day to day until it was as big as I. That was the second birth.

EVE Oh! That is too wonderful. It stirs inside me. It hurts.

THE SERPENT It nearly tore me asunder. Yet I am alive, and can burst my skin and renew myself as before. Soon there will be as many snakes in Eden as there are scales on my body. Then death will not matter: this snake and that snake will die; but the snakes will live.

EVE But the rest of us will die sooner or later, like the fawn. And then there will be nothing but snakes, snakes, snakes everywhere.

THE SERPENT That must not be. I worship you, Eve. I must have something to worship. Something quite different to myself, like you. There must be something greater than the snake.

EVE Yes: it must not be. Adam must not perish. You are very subtle: tell me what to do.

THE SERPENT Think. Will. Eat the dust. Lick the white stone: bite the apple you dread. The sun will give life.

EVE I do not trust the sun. I will give life myself. I will tear another Adam from my body if I tear my body to pieces in the act.

THE SERPENT Do. Dare it. Everything is possible; everything.

DORINDA   MRS SULLEN
young   young

The Beaux' Stratagem
George Farquhar

First performed in 1707 at the Queen's Theatre, London and set in Lichfield.

The main action concerns the adventures of the two 'beaux', Aimwell and Archer, who, in the guise of master and servant, travel up to Lichfield to recoup their broken fortunes, and succeed in carrying off the Squire's beautiful sister, Dorinda, and his wife, Mrs Sullen, who loathes her husband as much as he loathes her.

Having fallen in love with Dorinda at first sight, Aimwell contrives a meeting by pretending to fall sick outside the house of her mother, Lady Bountiful. He is carried inside by his 'manservant' Archer. When Aimwell has 'recovered' Lady Bountiful suggests that Dorinda shows him her collection of pictures. They are accompanied by Archer and Mrs Sullen. Dorinda and Aimwell soon wander off on their own, whilst Archer leads Mrs Sullen in the direction of her bedchamber.

In this scene, Dorinda and Mrs Sullen meet up to exchange confidences and compare their new 'beaux'.

Published by A&C Black, London

Act Four, Scene One

MRS SULLEN Well, sister!

DORINDA And well, sister!

MRS SULLEN What's become of my lord?

DORINDA What's become of his servant?

MRS SULLEN Servant! He's a prettier fellow, and a finer gentleman by fifty degrees, than his master.

DORINDA O'my conscience, I fancy you could beg that fellow at the gallows-foot!

MRS SULLEN O'my conscience, I could, provided I could put a friend of yours in his room.

DORINDA You desired me, sister, to leave you, when you transgressed the bounds of honour.

MRS SULLEN Thou dear censorious countrygirl! What dost mean? You can't think of the man without the bedfellow, I find.

DORINDA I don't find anything unnatural in that thought; while the mind is conversant with flesh and blood, it must conform to the humours of the company.

MRS SULLEN How a little love and good company improves a woman! Why, child, you begin to live – you never spoke before.

DORINDA Because I was never spoke to. – My lord has told me that I have more wit and beauty than any of my sex; and truly I begin to think the man is sincere.

MRS SULLEN You're in the right, Dorinda; pride is the life of a woman, and flattery is our daily bread; and she's a fool that won't believe a man there, as much as she that believes him in anything else. But I'll lay you a guinea that I had finer things said to me than you had.

DORINDA Done! What did your fellow say to ye?

MRS SULLEN My fellow took the picture of Venus for mine.

DORINDA But my lover took me for Venus herself.

MRS SULLEN Common cant! Had my spark[1] called me a Venus directly, I should have believed him a footman in good earnest.

DORINDA But my lover was upon his knees to me.

MRS SULLEN And mine was upon his tiptoes to me.

DORINDA Mine vowed to die for me.

MRS SULLEN Mine swore to die with me[2].

DORINDA Mine spoke the softest moving things.

MRS SULLEN Mine had his moving things too.

DORINDA Mine kissed my hand ten thousand times.

MRS SULLEN Mine has all that pleasure to come.

DORINDA Mine offered marriage.

MRS SULLEN O Lard! D'ye call that a moving thing?

DORINDA The sharpest arrow in his quiver, my dear sister! Why, my ten thousand pounds may lie brooding here this seven years, and hatch nothing at last but some ill-natured clown[3] like yours. Whereas, if I marry my Lord Aimwell, there will be title, place, and precedence, the park, the play, and the drawing-room, splendour, equipage, noise, and flambeaux[4]. – *Hey, my Lady Aimwell's servants there! – Lights, lights to the stairs! – My Lady Aimwell's coach put forward! – Stand by, make room for her ladyship!* – Are not these things moving? What! melancholy of a sudden?

MRS SULLEN Happy, happy sister! Your angel has been watchful for your happiness, whilst mine has slept regardless of his charge. Long smiling years of circling joys for you, but not one hour for me! [*Weeps.*]

DORINDA Come, my dear, we'll talk of something else.

MRS SULLEN Dorinda! I own myself a woman, full of my sex, a gentle, generous soul, easy and yielding to soft desires; a spacious heart, where love and all his train might lodge. And must the fair apartment of my breast be made a stable for a brute to lie in?

DORINDA Meaning your husband, I suppose?

MRS SULLEN Husband! No, even husband is too soft a name for him. – But come, I expect my brother here tonight or tomorrow; he was abroad when my father married me; perhaps he'll find a way to make me easy.

DORINDA Will you promise not to make yourself easy in the meantime with my lord's friend?

MRS SULLEN You mistake me, sister. It happens with us as among the men; the greatest talkers are the greatest cowards: and there's a reason for it; those spirits evaporate in prattle, which might do more mischief if they took another course. – Though, to confess the truth, I do love that fellow; – and if I met him dressed as he should be, and I undressed as I should be – look ye, sister, I have no supernatural gifts – I can't swear I could resist the temptation; though I can safely promise to avoid it; and that's as much as the best of us can do.

---

¹*spark* suitor, lover

²*to die with me* Mrs Sullen has in mind the very frequent meaning of 'die' in seventeenth- and eighteenth-century English – i.e., to reach sexual climax

³*clown* a country fellow, a rustic; also, an ungenteel or unmannerly person

⁴*flambeaux* torches

MARIE	CASSIE
30s	30s
Irish/North	Irish/North

Bold Girls

Rona Munro

First performed at the Cumberland Theatre, Strathclyde in 1991.

The play depicts the lives of three women, Nora, Cassie and Marie, living in war-torn Belfast. Although their men have been imprisoned and Marie's husband, Michael, has been killed, everyday life has to go on.

This scene is set in Marie's house after a girls' night out at the club. Nora has just left and Cassie pours herself another gin. Marie is gazing at Michael's picture. The remembrance of him warms her, but Cassie is about to shatter her illusions.

Published by Hodder & Stoughton, London

Scene Four

CASSIE How do you stand it here, Marie?

MARIE Sure where else would I go?

CASSIE How do you keep that smile on your face?

MARIE Super-glue.

CASSIE There's not one piece of bitterness in you, is there?

MARIE Oh Cassie.

CASSIE You see, you're good. And I'm just wicked.

MARIE Aye you're a bold woman altogether.

CASSIE Is it hard being good?

MARIE I took lessons.

CASSIE Well, tell me what you've got to smile about Marie, because I'm sure I can't see it.

MARIE I've a lot to be thankful for. I've my kids, a job, a nice wee house and I can still pay for it.

CASSIE You've two wee boys growing out of their clothes faster than you can get them new ones, a part-time job licking envelopes for a wage that wouldn't keep a budgie and three red bills on your mantelpiece there.

MARIE That's what's great about a Saturday out with you Cassie, you just know how to look at the bright side of things, don't you?

CASSIE Well just tell me how you can keep filling that kettle and making folk tea without pouring it over their head?

MARIE Ah well you see, I'm a mug.

CASSIE I think you are.

MARIE I didn't marry Joe, but . . .

CASSIE No. You did not. That mug was me.

MARIE See Cassie, I've had better times with Michael than a lot of women get in their whole lives with a man.

CASSIE And that keeps you going?

MARIE It's a warming kind of thought.

[*Cassie holds out her arms to Michael's pictures.*]

CASSIE [*singing*] 'Thanks – for the memories.'

MARIE Oh Cassie.

CASSIE That doesn't work, Marie. I've tried to keep myself warm that way. Find some man with good hands and a warm skin and wrap him round you to keep the rain off; you'll be damp in the end anyway.

MARIE Cassie, don't talk like that; you know you've not done half the wild things you make out.

CASSIE Not a quarter of what I've wanted to Marie, but enough to know it doesn't work. Grabbing onto some man because he smells like excitement, he smells like escape. They can't take you anywhere except into the back seat of their car. They're all the same.

MARIE If that's what you think of them that'll be all you'll find.

[*Cassie gets up to stand, looking at Michael.*]

CASSIE They are *all* the same, Marie.

MARIE No.

CASSIE No, not *Michael*. [*sarcastically*] Wasn't he just the perfect man, the perfect saint of a man.

MARIE He was no saint.

CASSIE He was not.

MARIE I never said he was a saint.

CASSIE Not much perfect about him.

MARIE We cared about each other! We were honest with each other!

CASSIE Honest!?

MARIE We were. He was a good man!

CASSIE Good!? He was a lying worm like every one of them!

[*There is a pause.*]

MARIE I think you should go home, Cassie.

CASSIE So he told you all about it did he? All the times he made a fool of you to your face?

MARIE Just go now.

CASSIE I don't believe you could have kept that smile on your face Marie, not if he was honestly telling you what he was up to.

MARIE Cassie . . .

CASSIE Making a fool of you with all those women.

[*There is a pause.*]

MARIE I heard the stories. Of course I heard them.

CASSIE Did you, though?

MARIE He was a great-looking man. He was away a lot. There were bound to be stories.

CASSIE There were books of them, Marie.

MARIE But if there'd been any truth in them Michael would've told me himself.

CASSIE Oh *Marie*!

MARIE That's trust Cassie!

CASSIE That's *stupidity*, Marie. You haven't the sense of a hen with its head off!

MARIE Michael would no more lie to me than you would, Cassie.

CASSIE Well we both did! That's what I'm telling you Marie! We were both lying to you for years!

YASMIN	AMINA
young	young

Borderline
Hanif Kureishi

First performed at the Royal Court Theatre in 1981.

Susan, a young journalist who has just returned from India, is gathering information for a radio programme about the Asian community in London. Among the younger people she talks to are Amina, daughter of Pakistani parents; Haroon, whose father owns the Light of India restaurant; and Anwar and Yasmin, organisers of the Asian Youth Movement. Amina and Haroon have been lovers for the past year, but now Haroon is going to university and Amina's father has arranged a suitable marriage for her.

In this scene, set in the park, Amina has been talking to Susan when Yasmin arrives. Yasmin has little time for journalists and Susan goes, leaving Amina and Yasmin on their own.

Published in *Outskirts and Other Plays* by Faber & Faber, London

Act Two, Scene Two

AMINA I like Susan. You're so hard on her.

YASMIN She's great fun.

AMINA What?

YASMIN Oh I've got no idea. She means well, yes.

AMINA Are you sad today?

YASMIN No, just thinking how to control an office full of angry, ignorant boys. They smoke and sweat and boil over. They talk of petrol bombs, they explain how to saw off a shotgun. I tell them to learn how to read and write. But they hate anything that takes longer than a night to achieve. Apparently they intend to do something about the stabbing. They're definitely not prepared to rely on either the police or prayer. [*Pause.*] Oh, I'm tired. I work so hard. And I can feel myself becoming too austere. Yes. When people do weak things they look guiltily at me. Or avoid me. Anwar.

AMINA I see.

YASMIN He is worried that weakness is capitulation. Stupid. I think I should fuck more.

AMINA Yes.

YASMIN What's Haroon like? No. Sorry.

AMINA Can I say something?

YASMIN If it's funny. [*Pause.*] No. What is it?

AMINA Suppose ... suppose you're in this situation. And you have to decide. You just have to. And if you did one thing you'd hurt people you love and nothing could be the same again. But if you did the other thing, what they want, you'd hurt yourself.

YASMIN How badly?

AMINA Badly. Badly.

YASMIN I won't decide things for you. You're too intelligent.

AMINA Yasmin, please.

YASMIN No.

AMINA Yes, you're right. I've decided already. I won't ...

YASMIN What?

AMINA I'm not going to resist.

YASMIN I see.

AMINA I'll marry him.

YASMIN There'd be just too much tearing of tissue all round, you mean.

AMINA My father.

YASMIN Him?

AMINA Yes.

YASMIN I've told you my own marriage wasn't a frolic.

AMINA Yasmin, can't you understand? I can't be tough like you. I just can't be. I can't. Sorry, I can't. I'm too frightened.

YASMIN Well.

AMINA Yasmin, tell me what to do.

YASMIN Go through with it then. For them.

AMINA It would be evil to defy them. You can't see that can you? What would I do with my freedom anyway. I don't think I can do good like you.

YASMIN Your father is too sick to defy.

AMINA Yes, yes.

YASMIN Go through it then. Then come out of it.

AMINA Could I?

YASMIN Maybe. In time.

AMINA I make you feel sick, I'm so weak. Don't you turn against me.

YASMIN I'd never do that.

AMINA You have already.

YASMIN Only a bit.

AMINA Oh, and this is silly. I'm not a virgin and I'm afraid my husband will complain to my father about it.

YASMIN Oh that. I tell you, you just scream at the right moment, that's an orgasm in itself for men. And beat their backs with your fists, tear their skin. When they complain say your passion overcame everything. And have no brats.

AMINA D'you know, the first time I met my future husband, Farouk, he picked his nose and wiped it on his tie.

YASMIN What kind of tie was it?

AMINA A big fish one. So bright he had to wear dark glasses.

YASMIN Do you like this weather?

AMINA I love it, yes.

YASMIN Do you? I always think the English talk too much about that stuff.

DORIS RUTTER   DOREEN BIDMEAD
40s   30s

Green Forms
(from *Office Suite*)
Alan Bennett

First transmitted on London Weekend Television in 1978 with
Patricia Routledge playing the part of Doreen and Prunella
Scales playing Doris.

Doris and Doreen work in an obscure department of a large
organisation in the North of England. Doreen is a married
lady in her thirties and Doris is unmarried in her forties and
lives with her elderly mother. Their office is cosy, if a little
run down, and they spend most of their time chatting, or
flirting with nice Mr Titmuss and carrying on a bitter feud
with Personnel. Today, however, is not a normal day and they
slowly begin to realise that their 'cushy little number' may be
coming to an end. Someone, somewhere in the organisation
has their eye on them and there are rumours of impending
redundancies.

In this opening scene, Doris is reading a newspaper and
Doreen sits contemplating her desk.

Published by Samuel French, London

DOREEN Are green forms still going through Mrs Henstridge?
[*Pause.*]
DORIS Newcastle.
DOREEN Newcastle?
DORIS Newcastle.
DOREEN You don't mean Manchester, Fordyce Road?
DORIS No. I mean Newcastle, Triad House.
DOREEN Then where's Mrs Henstridge? [*Pause.*] She was green
forms for as long as I can remember. And now you say it's
Newcastle. [*Pause.*] *Newcastle?*

DORIS Staff appointments and changes in personnel: Newcastle. [*The green form is inside an inter-office envelope. One look inside the envelope tells Doreen the form is green and therefore not their pigeon. If she does take the form out of the envelope she should not read it.*]

DOREEN Thin-faced woman. Blondeish. She had a son that wasn't right. Lived in Whingate.

DORIS I don't know where people live.

DOREEN Well, where's she gone and got to if she's not doing green forms? It used to be Southport.

DORIS It isn't Southport.

DOREEN I'm not saying it is Southport. Southport is being wound down.

DORIS Up.

DOREEN Up what?

DORIS Wound up.

DOREEN Wound down. Wound up. Phrased out anyway. I hope she hasn't been made ... you know ...

DORIS What?

DOREEN Well ... redundant. I wouldn't like to think she's been made redundant; she was very nicely spoken.

DORIS I never had the pleasure.

DOREEN Mrs Henstridge? Oh yes. You'll have gone up in the lift with her many a time. Smartish woman. Check costume. Brown swagger coat. [*She pauses.*] Fancy them phrasing out Southport. I never thought they'd phrase Southport out.
[*Pause.*]

DORIS Phasing, not phrasing.

DOREEN Come again?

DORIS Phasing. The phrase is phase. Not phrase.

DOREEN What did I say?

DORIS Phrasing.

DOREEN Oh. Well. If you'd come up to me ten years ago and said 'They're going to phase out Southport' I'd have laughed in your face.

DORIS You wouldn't.

DOREEN I would.

DORIS You wouldn't. If someone had come up to you ten years agao and said 'They're phasing out Southport', you wouldn't have known what they were talking about: you didn't work here then.
[*Pause.*]

DOREEN How's Mother?

DORIS Naught clever.

DOREEN No. I didn't think so, somehow.

DORIS Anyway, why single out Southport? I ran into Mr Butterfield in Planning and he says a question mark definitely hangs over Ipswich.

DOREEN Ipswich! That's only been going five years.

DORIS Four. She was on the commode half the night again.

DOREEN Poor lamb.

DORIS I think she must have eaten something. You can't turn your back. Last time it was the vicar. I just caught him doling her out the Milk Tray, else that would have been another three o'clock in the morning do. She's on a knife edge. People don't realize. One coffee cream and it's three months' devoted nursing down the drain. I'm trying to build her up.

DOREEN What I'm wondering is . . . Where will the axe fall next?

DORIS I know one thing. It won't fall on yours truly.

DOREEN Why not?

DORIS Because I'm Grade 3, that's why.

DOREEN Well I'm substantively Grade 3. Technically I'm Grade 4 but I'm holding down a Grade 3 job. If Central hadn't gone and frozen gradings I'd have been made up months since. Anyway I'm not going to worry: I've got Clifford.

DORIS Oh, Clifford.

DOREEN That's the thing about marriage, there's always the two of you.

DORIS There's two of Mother and me.

DOREEN We've talked it over and Cliff says that in the event of a real downturn in the economic climate he could fall back on the smallholding and me do my home hairdressing. People are always going to want their hair done, inflation or no inflation, and there's always a demand for rhubarb.

DORIS Yes. Well. I hope it keeps fine for you.

DOREEN 'Which twin has the Toni?' Remember? It's stood me in good stead has that. You don't catch me in a salon. Only you think it's Newcastle? This green form.

DORIS Newcastle.

DOREEN [*addressing the envelope; to herself*] Not . . . Mrs . . . Henstridge. Off you go to Newcastle. [*She takes it to the Out-tray by the door.*] We are getting on this morning. Proper little beavers. Oh, the *Bulletin*'s come. [*It is in the tray.*] You didn't tell me the *Bulletin* had come. [*She reads from the* Bulletin.]

'It's goodbye to Leeds, Cardigan Road. Smiles and sadness at simple ceremony.' Fancy shutting down Cardigan Road. That would have been unthinkable five years ago. It has its own canteen.

ZANDILE   LINDIWE
teenage   teenage
South African   South African

Have You Seen Zandile?

Gcina Mhlope, Maralin Vanrenen and Thembi Mtshali

First performed in 1986 at the Market Theatre, Johannesburg and also at the Edinburgh Festival in 1987 where it won the Fringe First Award.

At the beginning of the play Zandile is a child living with her grandmother in Durban. She is kidnapped by her mother and forced to conform to the ways of her harsh rural Transkei homeland.

In this scene it is December 1963 and Zandile, now a teenager, and her friend Lindiwe are preparing for a farewell party after finishing their final school examinations.

Published by Heinemann, New Hampshire/Methuen, London

Scene Thirteen
LINDIWE Zandi!
ZANDILE Yebo.
TOGETHER We did it! [*Laugh.*]
LINDIWE No more books.
ZANDILE No more swotting.
LINDIWE Matric is done forever. What if we don't pass?
ZANDILE Of course we'll pass, Lindiwe.
LINDIWE Anyway we can worry about that when the results come out next month.
ZANDILE But tomorrow . . .
TOGETHER It's a party. [*Laugh excitedly, and start singing.*] Oh what a night! Hey! Late December 1963. What a very special time for me . . . what a lady what a night! [*They collapse with laughter.*]
LINDIWE I have been waiting for this day!
ZANDILE But you are glad you came back, aren't you?

LINDIWE Aah, I had no choice . . . my parents forced me to come back.

ZANDILE They were right, you know, six months wasn't such a long time.

LINDIWE It's been too long for me because I want to see my Paul again.

ZANDILE Ever since you came back from that wedding, it's just Paul . . . Paul . . . Paul.

LINDIWE Because you don't know what happened to me the first time I saw Paul at the wedding ha!

ZANDILE Lindiwe, I have heard this a few million times now, I know your heart stopped and you started sweating just like in the Barbara Cartland books.

LINDIWE I can tell you this over and over.

ZANDILE Let me tell you what's going to make my heart stop . . . I'm worried . . . what are we presenting at the party tomorrow?

LINDIWE [*laughs*] Do you remember last year's party?

ZANDILE We were attending on last year's matrics. And were they boring!

LINDIWE And you . . . with the tray!

ZANDILE Don't remind me please.

LINDIWE You were walking along with the big tray.

ZANDILE Yes. There were twenty-four plastic cups filled with Coca-Cola.

LINDIWE For the twelve prefects and their partners.

ZANDILE I remember the tune that was playing: 'Papa was a Rolling Stone'. As I was walking nicely along to the music with the tray then that stupid clumsy Zola danced right into me!

LINDIWE Nonsense! You tripped. Those shoes you had on were too tight. Why is it your shoes were always too small for you?

ZANDILE This boy danced right into me and over I went, on to the headboy's lap and his girlfriend, I forget her name now . . .

LINDIWE Caroline.

ZANDILE [*imitating Caroline in Zulu*] 'I always knew you had your eyes on Sipho.'

LINDIWE As if you were so desperate.

ZANDILE Meanwhile my eyes were on the floor.

LINDIWE And there was Coca-Cola everywhere, all over the pretty pink and blue and . . .

ZANDILE Yellow.

LINDIWE Dresses were ruined. I laughed. You! Your face was blushing.

ZANDILE Everybody was so sticky and so cross.

LINDIWE Ah, but at least it woke them up.

ZANDILE Let's stop laughing at other people. What are we going to do tomorrow?

LINDIWE Maybe we can do a song Paul taught me.

ZANDILE Paul again. Lindiwe, this Paul is haunting us now. Who invented telephones? Paul. Who discovered the sea route to India? Paul ... Paul. [*Mocking.*]

LINDIWE You are jealous.

ZANDILE Okay, let's do his song. What is it?

LINDIWE 'Sugar Sugar'.

ZANDILE Does that mean I'm going to be your sugar sugar tomorrow? [*Laughs.*]

LINDIWE Haai suka wena! [*She starts singing and dancing.*] Sugar Sugar ...

ZANDILE And what do I sing?

LINDIWE Pa pum pa pum ...

ZANDILE Pa pum pa pum ... Okay let's try.

LINDIWE Sugar Sugar ...

ZANDILE Pa pum pa pum ...

LINDIWE Oh, honey honey ...

ZANDILE Pa pa pum ... [*Lindiwe stares at the way Zandile is dancing and stops singing in horror.*]

LINDIWE You can't dance like this. Oh, they will laugh at you – you must shake like this! [*She shows Zandile.*]

ZANDILE Well, you must teach me Lindiwe.

LINDIWE Sugar Sugar ... [*Shaking.*]

ZANDILE Pa pum pa pum ...

LINDIWE Oh, honey honey ...

ZANDILE Pa pum pa pum ...

LINDIWE [*stops again*] Zandile ... haai haai ... your shoulders! Ezase Jo'burg!

ZANDILE Alright – siyafunda eJo'burg!

LINDIWE Sugar Sugar ...

ZANDILE Pa pum pa pum ...

LINDIWE Oh, honey honey ...

ZANDILE Pa pum pa pum ...

LINDIWE Your knees ... go down! Sugar Sugar ...

ZANDILE Pa pum pa pum ...

LINDIWE Your knees ... Sugar Sugar ...

ZANDILE Pa pum pa pum ...

LINDIWE Oh, honey honey ... (*Zandile is concentrating on her knees and forgets to sing.*]

LINDIWE And sing at the same time! You are my candy girl ...

ZANDILE Hey?

LINDIWE And you got me wanting you! [*They laugh and exclaim in Xhosa: 'We'll show them.'*]

ZANDILE I like this, but is this all your Paul does? He doesn't work he just sings sugar sugar to you all day long? That's marriage material.

LINDIWE Suka! He does work.

ZANDILE What does he do?

LINDIWE He plays drums.

ZANDILE You call that work?

LADY CHILTERN   MRS CHEVELEY
27   late 20s

An Ideal Husband
Oscar Wilde

This 'society comedy' was first produced in 1895 at the Haymarket Theatre, London.

The play is set mainly in the Grosvenor Square home of Sir Robert Chiltern, respected politican and Under-Secretary for Foreign Affairs. He and Lady Chiltern are entertaining guests. One of these guests is the fascinating but unscrupulous Mrs Cheveley.

During the evening Mrs Cheveley contrives to speak to Sir Robert privately. She has a large investment in the Argentine Canal scheme, which Sir Robert has publicly denounced as a swindle. She informs him that it will be in his interest to reconsider his opinion and withdraw his report on the matter. If he refuses, she has information in her possession that will ruin him. The following morning Mrs Cheveley receives a note from Sir Robert refusing to accede to her demands, and in this scene she confronts Lady Chiltern.

Published by A&C Black, London

Act Two

MRS CHEVELEY Wonderful woman, Lady Markby, isn't she? Talks more and says less than anybody I ever met. She is made to be a public speaker. Much more so than her husband, though he is a typical Englishman, always dull and usually violent.

LADY CHILTERN [*Makes no answer, but remains standing. There is a pause. Then the eyes of the two women meet. Lady Chiltern looks stern and pale. Mrs Cheveley seems rather amused.*]
Mrs Cheveley, I think it is right to tell you quite frankly that, had I known who you really were, I should not have invited you to my house last night.

MRS CHEVELEY [*with an impertinent smile*] Really?

LADY CHILTERN I could not have done so.

MRS CHEVELEY I see that after all these years you have not changed a bit, Gertrude.

LADY CHILTERN I never change.

MRS CHEVELEY [*elevating her eyebrows*] Then life has taught you nothing?

LADY CHILTERN It has taught me that a person who has once been guilty of a dishonest and dishonourable action may be guilty of it a second time, and should be shunned.

MRS CHEVELEY Would you apply that rule to everyone?

LADY CHILTERN Yes, to everyone, without exception.

MRS CHEVELEY Then I am sorry for you, Gertrude, very sorry for you.

LADY CHILTERN You see now, I am sure, that for many reasons any further acquaintance between us during your stay in London is quite impossible?

MRS CHEVELEY [*leaning back in her chair*] Do you know, Gertrude, I don't mind your talking morality a bit. Morality is simply the attitude we adopt towards people whom we personally dislike. You dislike me. I am quite aware of that. And I have always detested you. And yet I have come here to do you a service.

LADY CHILTERN [*contemptuously*] Like the service you wished to render my husband last night, I suppose. Thank heaven, I saved him from that.

MRS CHEVELEY [*starting to her feet*] It was you who made him write that insolent letter to me? It was you who made him break his promise?

LADY CHILTERN Yes.

MRS CHEVELEY Then you must make him keep it. I give you till tomorrow morning – no more. If by that time your husband does not solemnly bind himself to help me in this great scheme in which I am interested—

LADY CHILTERN This fraudulent speculation—

MRS CHEVELEY Call it what you choose. I hold your husband in the hollow of my hand, and if you are wise you will make him do what I tell him.

LADY CHILTERN [*rising and going towards her*] You are impertinent. What has my husband to do with you? With a woman like you?

MRS CHEVELEY [*with a bitter laugh*] In this world like meets with like. It is because your husband is himself fraudulent and dishonest that we pair so well together. Between you and him there are chasms. He and I are closer than friends. We are enemies linked together. The same sin binds us.

LADY CHILTERN How dare you class my husband with yourself? How dare you threaten him or me? Leave my house. You are unfit to enter it.

[*Sir Robert Chiltern enters from behind. He hears his wife's last words, and sees to whom they are addressed. He grows deadly pale.*]

MRS CHEVELEY Your house! A house bought with the price of dishonour. A house, everything in which has been paid for by fraud. [*Turns round and sees Sir Robert Chiltern.*] Ask him what the origin of his fortune is! Get him to tell you how he sold to a stockbroker a Cabinet secret. Learn from him to what you owe your position.

LADY CHILTERN It is not true! Robert! It is not true!

MRS CHEVELEY [*pointing at him with outstretched finger*] Look at him! Can he deny it? Does he dare to?

ALICE MCNAUGHT
34

MRS MERCY CROFT
of indeterminate age

The Killing of Sister George
Frank Marcus

First performed at the Duke of York's Theatre, London in 1965.

Sister George is the main character in *Applehurst* – a long-running radio serial about village life. Now the time has come for 'George' to be 'killed off' and Mrs Mercy Croft, Assistant Head of BBC serials, has been sent to break the news to middle-aged actress June Buckridge, who has played the part for over two thousand performances.

June has also been involved in a long-term lesbian relationship with her flatmate, the child-like Alice McNaught – obsessed with her collection of dolls and one in particular called Emmeline. The relationship is becoming increasingly strained now that June is losing her job, and Alice, easily lured by promises of working as private secretary to Mercy Croft, makes up her mind to leave.

In this scene Mercy is waiting for her with outstretched arms. Alice runs over to her, and laying her head on Mercy's shoulder, bursts into tears.

Published by Samuel French, London

Act Three

MERCY My poor child. There, there.
ALICE I can't stand it any more.
MERCY I know, I know. You've been under a terrible strain.
ALICE [*breaking from Mercy*] You've no idea, Mrs Mercy.
MERCY I can imagine.
ALICE She's been *terrible!*
MERCY Hush, dear. She'll hear you. [*She leads Alice to the sofa.*]
   [*Alice sits on the sofa. Mercy sits R of Alice.*]
ALICE I was praying you'd come.

MERCY I wasn't going to leave you alone with her today. [*She smiles.*] Besides – I had promised.

ALICE Oh, I know, but I knew how busy you were.

MERCY First things first.

ALICE I knew I could rely on you. I felt it the first time I met you.

MERCY And I felt I was speaking to a proud and sensitive person, whose personality was being systematically crushed.

ALICE [*turning away*] Don't!

MERCY And with a definite literary talent.

ALICE [*turning*] Honestly? Do you really think so?

MERCY I'm being quite objective.

ALICE Gosh! Wouldn't it be marvellous!

MERCY What, dear?

ALICE If I could do some work for you – writing, I mean.

MERCY We shall see what transpires. I'll certainly give you all the help I can.

ALICE Oh, you are nice.

MERCY And the other offer still stands.

ALICE [*looking away*] Yes, well – I think I've almost definitely decided. I'm sorry to be so vague.

MERCY [*after a pause*] Not at all. [*She rises and moves up R of the sofa.*]

ALICE It's a bit of a wrench, you know. I've been working for Mr Katz for nearly four years. I'd have to give him a month's notice.

MERCY [*moving above the sofa*] There's no rush. I told you I'd keep the job open for a fortnight.

ALICE And then there's George.

MERCY [*with a glance up L*] Yes.

ALICE I mean: I don't know how she'd take it.

MERCY [*moving to L of the sofa*] You have told her, of course?

ALICE God, no! She'd have murdered me.
[*Mercy crosses to the table LC, stands with her back to the audience and pours a cup of tea.*]

MERCY In view of what happened today, I think we were very wise.

ALICE If she suspected I'd been to see you behind her back ...

MERCY There was no reason why you shouldn't. You're perfectly entitled ...

ALICE Oh, I *know*. But she's so possessive. I'm never allowed anywhere near the BBC. I'm kept a guilty secret.

MERCY She's shackled you to her. [*She sits R of the table LC.*] Anyway, you wouldn't be working for the BBC. You'd be working for me as my own private secretary, in my London flat.

ALICE [*rising and crossing to R of Mercy*] It sounds absolutely super. I'm sorry I'm being so slow about making up my mind.

MERCY A thought has just occurred to me: if you're in any kind of trouble – you know, with George – you can always camp down at the flat. There's a divan . . .

ALICE Oh, that'd be *wonderful!*

MERCY It could serve as your temporary HQ. It's not luxurious, mind. [*She drinks her tea.*]

ALICE Never mind that. It would be an escape – if necessary.

MERCY That's what I thought. I only ever stay there myself if I've been kept late at a story conference, or something like that. I find it useful. I suppose it's a place for me to escape, too.

ALICE [*after a pause*] We'd be like prisoners on the run.

[*There is a pause. Mercy drinks then puts down her cup.*]

MERCY Do you really think you can escape?

ALICE [*after a pause*] I don't know. [*She moves up C and glances off L.*]

MERCY It's very difficult for you.

ALICE [*moving up R*] It's been so long, so many years. [*She picks up Emmeline from the table behind the sofa.*]

MERCY It's hard to break the routine.

ALICE It's the little things one misses most.

MERCY [*smiling*] You could bring your dolls.

ALICE [*moving to the armchair R and hugging Emmeline*] I couldn't go anywhere without them. I even take them on holiday – and then I'm terrified they'll get lost or stolen. Sometimes George hides them – it's her idea of a joke.

MERCY A very cruel joke.

[*Alice, still holding the doll, runs to Mercy and kneels R of her.*]

ALICE Don't let her get at me, Mrs Mercy. Stay here – don't go away. [*She clutches Mercy's knees.*]

MERCY I can't stay here all day, dear.

ALICE Please don't leave me. I'm terrified of what she will do.

MERCY Calm yourself, Alice. No one's going to hurt you. Here, put your head on my shoulder.

[*Alice lays her head on Mercy's shoulder.*]

Close your eyes. Relax. My goodness, you're trembling like a leaf. [*She strokes Alice's hair.*]

ALICE [*with her eyes shut*] That's nice.

MERCY You're my little girl. You're going to be – my little girl.

EVA
17
English

HELGA
middle-aged
German

Kindertransport

Diane Samuels

First produced by the Soho Theatre Company at the Cockpit Theatre, London in 1993 and at the Vaudeville Theatre in 1996.

Between 1938 and 1939 nearly ten thousand children, mostly Jewish, were sent from Germany to Britian. One of these children, Eva Schlesinger, arrives in Manchester, expecting her parents to join her later. When her parents fail to escape the holocaust she changes her name to Evelyn and begins the process of denying her roots ...

In this scene Eva is 17. Her mother, Helga, having survived the concentration camp, meets her daughter again after seven years. She is utterly transformed: thin, wizened and old-looking. She hopes to take Eva to America to start a new life, but Eva, now known as Evelyn, is reluctant to go with her once beloved 'mutti'.

Published by Nick Hern Books, London

Act Two, Scene One

HELGA Ist das Eva? (Is it Eva?).

[*Eva is speechless.*]

HELGA Eva, bist du's wirklich? (Is that you, Eva?)

EVA Mother?

[*Helga approaches Eva and hugs her. Eva tries to hug back but is clearly very uncomfortable.*]

HELGA Wie du dich verändert hast! (How much you have changed!)

EVA I'm sorry. I don't quite understand.

HELGA How much you have changed.

EVA So have you.

HELGA You are sixteen now.

EVA Seventeen.

HELGA Blue is suiting to you. A lovely dress.

EVA Thank you.

HELGA You are very pretty.

EVA This is a nice hotel. I can't believe you're here.

HELGA I promised I would come, Eva.

EVA I'm called Evelyn now.

HELGA What is Evelyn?

EVA I changed my name.

HELGA Why?

EVA I wanted an English name.

HELGA Eva was the name of your great grandmother.

EVA I didn't mean any disrespect.

HELGA No. Of course not.

EVA I'm sorry.

HELGA Nothing is the same any more.

EVA It's just that I've settled down now.

HELGA These are the pieces of my life.

EVA There were no letters for all those years and then I saw the newsreels and newspapers . . .

HELGA I am putting them all back together again.

EVA I thought the worst.

HELGA I always promised that I would come and get you.

EVA I was a little girl then.

HELGA I am sorry that there has been such a delay. It was not of my making. [*Pause.*] I am your mutti, Eva.

EVA Evelyn.

HELGA Eva. Now I am here, you have back your proper name.

EVA Evelyn is on my naturalisation papers.

HELGA Naturalised as English?

EVA And adopted by Mr and Mrs Miller.

HELGA How can you be adopted when your own mother is alive for you?

EVA I thought that you were not alive.

HELGA Never mind it. We have all done bad things in the last years that we regret. That is how we survive.

EVA What did you do?

HELGA I was right to send you here, yes? It is good to survive. Is it not, Eva?

EVA Please call me Evelyn.

HELGA Now we must put our lives right again. We will go to New York where your Onkel Klaus will help us to make a beginning.

EVA All the way to New York?

HELGA Who is here for us? No one. The remains of our family is in America.

EVA I have a family here.

HELGA These people were just a help to you in bad times. You can leave them now behind. The bad times are finished. I know it.

EVA I like it here.

HELGA You will like it better in America.

EVA Do I have to go away with you?

HELGA That is what I came for.

CÉCILE VOLANGES   MARQUISE DE MERTEUIL
15

Les Liaisons Dangereuses
Christopher Hampton

First performed by the Royal Shakespeare Company at The
Other Place, Stratford-upon-Avon in 1985 and later transferred
to the Barbican Theatre, London.

The action takes place in Paris in the 1780s and revolves
around the planned seduction of young Cécile Volanges, fresh
from her convent school, and the demure Mme de Tourvel by
the cynical, pleasure-seeking Vicomte de Valmont. He is
encouraged in both these enterprises by his former mistress,
the dangerous Marquise de Merteuil. Cécile's mother has
arranged for her to marry Gercourt, who is away with his
regiment in Corsica. Merteuil befriends Cécile but, unknown
to her, she has already alerted Mme Volanges to her daughter's
secret attachment to young Danceny.

In this scene, Cécile, looking distraught and exhausted,
breaks down and confesses to Merteuil that she foolishly gave
Valmont the key to her room so that he could bring her letters
from Danceny without her mother's knowledge. But Valmont
has used this opportunity to seduce her and has even arranged
to visit her again the next night.

Published by Faber & Faber, London

Act One, Scene Seven

MERTEUIL My dear, I really can't help you unless you tell me
what's troubling you.

CÉCILE I can't, I just can't.

MERTEUIL I thought we'd agreed not to keep any secrets from
one another.

CÉCILE I'm so unhappy.

[*Cécile bursts into tears. Merteuil takes her in her arms and
soothes her mechanically, her expression, as long as it's not
seen by Cécile, bored and impatient.*]

Everything's gone wrong since the day Maman found Danceny's letters.

MERTEUIL Yes, that was very stupid of you. How could you have let that happen?

CÉCILE Someone must have told her, she went straight to my bureau and opened the drawer I was keeping them in.

MERTEUIL Who could have done such a thing?

CÉCILE It must have been my chambermaid ...

MERTEUIL Or your confessor perhaps?

CÉCILE Oh, no, surely not.

MERTEUIL You can't always trust those people, my dear.

CÉCILE That's terrible.

MERTEUIL But today, what is the matter today?

CÉCILE You'll be angry with me.

MERTEUIL Are you sure you don't want me to be angry with you?

[*Cécile looks up at Merteuil, surprised by the acuteness of this idea.*]

Come along.

CÉCILE I don't know how to speak the words.

MERTEUIL Perhaps I am beginning to get angry.

[*Merteuil has spoken quietly: and now there's a long silence. Finally, Cécile takes a deep breath.*]

CÉCILE Last night ...

MERTEUIL Yes.

CÉCILE So that we could exchange letters to and from Danceny without arousing suspicions, I gave Monsieur de Valmont the key to my bedroom ...

MERTEUIL Yes.

CÉCILE And last night he used it. I thought he'd just come to bring me a letter. But he hadn't. And by the time I realized what he had come for, it was, well, it was too late to stop him ...

[*Cécile bursts into tears again; but this time Merteuil doesn't take her in her arms. Instead, she considers her coolly for a moment before speaking.*]

MERTEUIL You mean to tell me you're upset because Monsieur de Valmont has taught you something you've undoubtedly been dying to learn?

[*Cécile's tears are cut off and she looks up in shock.*]

CÉCILE What?

MERTEUIL And am I to understand that what generally brings a girl to her senses has deprived you of yours?

CÉCILE I thought you'd be horrified.

MERTEUIL Tell me: you resisted him, did you?

CÉCILE Of course I did, as much as I could.

MERTEUIL But he forced you?

CÉCILE It wasn't that exactly, but I found it almost impossible to defend myself.

MERTEUIL Why was that? Did he tie you up?

CÉCILE No, no, but he has a way of putting things, you just can't think of an answer.

MERTEUIL Not even no?

CÉCILE I kept saying no, all the time: but somehow that wasn't what I was doing. And in the end ...

MERTEUIL Yes?

CÉCILE I told him he could come back tonight.
[*Silence. Cécile seems, once again, trembling on the edge of tears.*]
I'm so ashamed.

MERTEUIL You'll find the shame is like the pain: you only feel it once.

CÉCILE And this morning it was terrible. As soon as I saw Maman, I couldn't help it, I burst into tears.

MERTEUIL I'm surprised you missed the opportunity to bring the whole thing to a rousing climax by confessing all. You wouldn't be worrying about tonight if you'd done that; you'd be packing your bags for the convent.

CÉCILE What am I going to do?

MERTEUIL You really want my advice?

CÉCILE Please.
[*Merteuil considers a moment.*]

MERTEUIL Allow Monsieur de Valmont to continue your instruction. Convince your mother you have forgotten Danceny. And raise no objection to the marriage.
[*Cécile gapes at Merteuil, bewildered.*]

CÉCILE With Monsieur de Gercourt?

MERTEUIL When it comes to marriage one man is as good as the next; and even the least accommodating is less trouble than a mother.

CÉCILE But what about Danceny?

MERTEUIL He seems patient enough; and once you're married, you should be able to see him without undue difficulty.

CÉCILE I thought you once said to me, I'm sure you did, one evening at the Opéra, that once I was married, I would have to be faithful to my husband.

MERTEUIL Your mind must have been wandering, you must have been listening to the opera.

CÉCILE So, are you saying I'm going to have to do that with three different men?

MERTEUIL I'm saying, you stupid little girl, that provided you take a few elementary precautions, you can do it, or not, with as many men as you like, as often as you like, in as many different ways as you like. Our sex has few enough advantages, you may as well make the most of those you have. Now here comes your mama, so remember what I've said and, above all, no more snivelling.

CÉCILE Yes, Madame.

NELL GWYN   LIZ FARLEY
16   young

Playhouse Creatures
April de Angelis

First performed by the Sphinx Company at the Haymarket
Studio, Leicester in 1993, opening later that year at the Lyric
Studio, Hammersmith, London.

The play is set in Restoration London and follows the lives
of five actresses, one of them the famous Nell Gwyn, and
their struggle against the threat of poverty and pestilence.

In this early scene, Nell, working as a barmaid at the Cock
and Pie, meets Liz Farley, a young street preacher who is
desperately trying to convert an unreceptive audience.

Published by Samuel French, London

Act One, Scene Two

MRS FARLEY And lo
  It is written in our Lord's book
  That this time shall come to pass.
  And ye have only to look about ye and ye will see
  that it has come to pass.
  Yes, it hath.
  [*Nell enters, as if from a pub doorway. She holds a jug.*]
NELL [*calling in*] All right! All right! In a bleedin' minute! [*She
  sighs in exasperation and sits down.*]
MRS FARLEY Ye shall see that the cows do not give sweet milk
  but are dry except for stinking curdles.
  Ye shall find all men to be cheats and their hair
  to be lice riddled.
  Yeah, ye shall discover even the women at your hearth
  to be fornicators!
NELL [*calling in once more*] I'm having a fucking break!
MRS FARLEY And a great plague of locusts will settle in the fields
  and pester your cows ... [*She starts to cry.*]

NELL You crying? Don't take it personal. I always shout.

MRS FARLEY Usually I take round the hat. Just then I was making it up. Could you tell?

NELL Seemed all right.

MRS FARLEY He was my dad, the preacher. It was last rites all summer with the plague. He said God was protecting him. And then, just last week, when it seemed to be over, the boils came up. Purple. Behind his knees. This morning thought I better just carry on. You know. This was our spot.
[*Pause.*]
There's a lot of work to be done. Stamping out heathen decadence.

NELL How much did you get today, then? Stamping.

MRS FARLEY Well . . .

NELL Go on.

MRS FARLEY I've not earnt a penny. What am I going to do? I could starve!

NELL That's 'cos you don't know how to work a crowd. I sold oysters with me sister. We had a patter. Crowds like patter.

MRS FARLEY A patter?

NELL You know: 'Oyster sucking's better than—'

MRS FARLEY [*interrupting*] We spread God's plain and holy word.

NELL It's like you've got to have a bit of cunning.

MRS FARLEY Cunning?

NELL To get what you want.

MRS FARLEY I'm not sure. I think cunning is against my religion.

NELL God helps those who help themselves. I got meself a job at the Cock and Pie.

MRS FARLEY I've heard about places like that.

NELL I serve strong waters to the gentlemen.

MRS FARLEY I've heard it's the devil's own armpit.

NELL It has a decent, reg'lar sort of clientele.
[*A bellow is heard from the Cock and Pie.*]
On the whole. You do get the odd difficult customer. There's one bloke won't take no for an answer. I told him I wouldn't go with him. Not for sixpence. I know where he's been.

MRS FARLEY Where's that?

NELL With me sister, and she'd do anybody.

MRS FARLEY Well, I better go.

NELL Where?

MRS FARLEY It's four o'clock. That's when I used to wash my
dad's collars.

NELL No point washing 'em now. You never liked washing 'em,
did you?

[*Pause.*]

MRS FARLEY No.

[*They laugh.*]

It's only I can't think what else to do.

[*Pause.*]

NELL Do you know poetry? I'll give you sixpence if you teach
me a bit poetry.

MRS FARLEY Poetry?

NELL Can you say it?

MRS FARLEY 'The angel of the Lord came down and glory shone
around.'

NELL Brilliant.

[*Nell gives her sixpence. Mrs Farley takes it.*]

That a deal then? You won't starve now.

MRS FARLEY Not today. Why do you want to know poetry?

NELL For a job.

MRS FARLEY At the Cock and Pie?

NELL No. Across the street. The playhouse.

MRS FARLEY The playhouse! That den of defilement! That pit of
pestilence!

NELL I've seen the ladies. They've got lovely dresses.

MRS FARLEY Have they?

NELL I've crept in the back. The candlelight shines their hair so
their hair seems like flames. Glittering buckles on their shoes.
Gold lace dresses.

MRS FARLEY Lace! Do they fornicate?

NELL Fuck knows. They speak poetry and walk about. [*She
demonstrates, speaking in a posh voice.*]

'Oysters, oysters, by the shell or by the cup.

Slide 'em down your gullet to keep your pecker up.'

MRS FARLEY And they want ladies?

NELL Just one.

MRS FARLEY Just one. Oh.

NELL I heard 'em talking. In the pub. Teach me now.

MRS FARLEY I need to fetch things. A book of poetry. From my
lodgings.

NELL I'll come with you.

MRS FARLEY No. It's not far. You wait. I'll meet you back here.

[*She moves to the exit.*]

NELL I'll wait then. [*She calls after her.*] Here, I don't know your name.

MRS FARLEY Elizabeth. Elizabeth Farley.

NELL And I'm Nellie. Nellie Gwyn.

[*Mrs Farley exits. Nell goes over to the pub and shouts in.*] You can stuff your poxy job! [*She waits. She talks to herself.*] They want a lady. Lady Nell. Oysters . . . oysters . . . and glory shone around. You need a patter. It's like you've got to have a bit of cunning. Cunning? [*She jumps up and looks about her.*] Fuck. I've been bleedin' had.

MIRANDA

PAULA
young
London

The Positive Hour
April de Angelis

First performed by Out of Joint at Hampstead Theatre, London in 1997.

Miranda is a social worker with no shortage of problems. Not the least of these is Paula, an unemployed single mother who has taken up prostitution to survive and whose 8-year-old daughter, Victoria, is in foster care.

The play opens in Miranda's office. It is her first day back at work after her 'nervous collapse'. She is confronted by a distraught Paula, demanding that her daughter be returned to her immediately.

Published by Faber & Faber, London

Act One, Scene One

PAULA I don't want any more bollocks.

MIRANDA Pardon?

PAULA Bollocks.

MIRANDA Now, Paula ...

PAULA I'm a desperate woman. You must've seen one of us before? We smoke and have hastily applied mascara. It's my daughter. Victoria Savage. Eight and three-quarters. Her favourite groups are Spice Girls and Michael Jackson. I haven't got the heart to tell her he's a pervert. I mean, children are in their own special world, aren't they?

MIRANDA I've got your file here.

PAULA Temporarily fostered with the Clements. Mr and Mrs Patrick of Sussex. They don't like me going there. They say it upsets Victoria. Course it does. I'm her mother. It's a wrench when I leave. She cries, I cry. It's a fucking mess. Patrick's a bank manager and Isobel doesn't know what to do with herself. They have a mug tree. Know the sort? Victoria's a very demanding child. That house was dead and now they're wetting themselves with having a bit of life in their life, but it's my fucking bit of life.

MIRANDA Paula, fostering is a temporary arrangement and every effort is made to return the child to its mother.

PAULA So they say.

MIRANDA This is my first morning, Paula. You probably know that I've been away for a bit. I just wanted the opportunity to meet you and to discuss your situation.

PAULA You see, this thing has happened in their heads. Somehow they think they are Victoria's parents and I am a passing annoyance.

MIRANDA I'm sure that's not the case.

PAULA And people are going to look at them and look at me and think she's better off with them. But she's my daughter.

MIRANDA A child is always better off with its mother unless there are serious concerns for its welfare.

PAULA Do you like me?

MIRANDA I haven't introduced myself. Miranda Hurst.

PAULA Because it's important, isn't it, Miranda, that you like me? What you think is important?

MIRANDA My assessment will have a bearing on the outcome of your case, but it would be bad practice if I let personal opinion interfere with professional judgement.

PAULA So what are you going to do about Victoria?

MIRANDA Well, there's nothing I can do today.

PAULA No one's listening to me.

MIRANDA Of course we want to place your daughter back with you. That's terribly important, but what we have to do is to see that as a goal at the end of a longer term process.

PAULA A process?

MIRANDA Yes.

PAULA Five months now they've had her.

MIRANDA Yes, Paula.

PAULA So how long's a process?

MIRANDA It's as long as it takes.

PAULA I'm sick of people keep putting me off.

MIRANDA Paula . . .

PAULA Don't fucking Paula me. [*She pulls a razor blade out of her bag and holds it to her wrist.*] Don't even fucking move.

MIRANDA Please, Paula, put that away.

PAULA I'm never happy, not without Victoria. I wake up in the morning and it's like there's a big hole in my chest only I'm too scared to look down because once I do I'm going to feel this pain.

MIRANDA It must be very hard. Now, please, let's be calm.

PAULA No. Let's be hysterical. Let's have blood.

MIRANDA Of course we must start the whole thing moving now.

PAULA Moving, that's good, Miranda.

MIRANDA Because, believe me, I want your daughter to be given back to you very much. The problems are solvable. I will have failed if we don't get Victoria back with you and I don't want to fail. Why don't you sit down and put that away and then we can begin.

[*Pause. Paula sits down and places the blade near to her on the desk between them.*]

PAULA I'm putting it here.

MIRANDA Actually I had a sort of collapse. An exhaustion thing. After six months my doctor said, 'Yes, go back to work, but avoid stressful situations.' This is my first day.

PAULA Oh. Sorry.

[*Miranda opens Paula's file.*]

MIRANDA We think it was a virus.

PAULA There's a lot of weird things about.

MIRANDA Well. I'd just like to go over a few details to start with.

ROSE   SYBIL
young

The Shoemaker's Holiday
Thomas Dekker

This London comedy was probably first performed at the Rose Theatre, London in the late summer of 1599.

It tells the story of Simon Eyre, a shoemaker, who through his hard work and popularity becomes Lord Mayor of London. At the beginning of the play, Roland Lacy, nephew of the Earl of Lincoln and later employed by Eyre as 'Hans', a Dutch shoemaker, is being sent to join the army in France.

In this scene, his sweetheart, Rose, daughter of the present Lord Mayor, is lamenting Lacy's absence and making a garland for his head when her spirited maid, Sybil, comes in bringing news of Lacy from London.

Published by A&C Black, London

Scene Two

ROSE Here sit thou down upon this flow'ry bank,
   And make a garland for thy Lacy's head.
   These pinks, these roses, and these violets,
   These blushing gilliflowers, these marigolds,
   The fair embroidery of his coronet,
   Carry not half such beauty in their cheeks
   As the sweet countenance of my Lacy doth.
   O my most unkind father! O my stars,
   Why loured you so at my nativity
   To make me love, yet live robbed of my love?
   Here as a thief am I imprisonèd
   For my dear Lacy's sake, within those walls
   Which by my father's cost were builded up
   For better purposes. Here must I languish
   For him that doth as much lament, I know,
   Mine absence as for him I pine in woe.

[*Enter Sybil.*]

SYBIL Good morrow, young mistress. I am sure you make that garland for me, against I shall be Lady of the Harvest.

ROSE Sybil, what news at London?

SYBIL None but good. My Lord Mayor your father, and Master Philpot your uncle, and Master Scott your cousin, and Mistress Frigbottom by Doctors' Commons[1], do all, by my troth, send you most hearty commendations.

ROSE Did Lacy send kind greetings to his love?

SYBIL O yes, out of cry[2]. By my troth, I scant knew him – here 'a wore a scarf, and here a scarf, here a bunch of feathers, and here precious stones and jewels, and a pair of garters – O monstrous! – like one of our yellow silk curtains at home here in Old Ford House, here in Master Bellymount's chamber. I stood at our door in Cornhill, looked at him, he at me indeed; spake to him, but he not to me, not a word. Marry gup[3], thought I, with a wanion[4]! He passed by me as proud – Marry, foh! Are you grown humorous[5]? thought I – and so shut the door, and in I came.

ROSE O Sybil, how dost thou my Lacy wrong!
My Roland is as gentle as a lamb,
No dove was ever half so mild as he.

SYBIL Mild? Yea, as a bushel[6] of stamped crabs[7]! He looked upon me as sour as verjuice[8]. Go thy ways, thought I, thou mayst be much in my gaskins, but nothing in my netherstocks[9]. This is your fault, mistress, to love him that loves not you. He thinks scorn to do as he's done to, but if I were as you,
I'd cry: go by, Jeronimo[10], go by!
I'd set mine old debts against my new driblets[11],
And the hare's foot against the goose giblets[12];
For if ever I sigh[13] when sleep I should take,
Pray God I may lose my maidenhead when I wake.

ROSE Will my love leave me then and go to France?

SYBIL I know not that, but I am sure I see him stalk before the soldiers. By my troth, he is a proper[14] man, but he is proper that proper doth. Let him go snick up[15], young mistress.

ROSE Get thee to London, and learn perfectly
Whether my Lacy go to France or no.
Do this, and I will give thee for thy pains
My cambric apron, and my Romish gloves,
My purple stockings, and a stomacher.
Say, wilt thou do this, Sybil, for my sake?

SYBIL Will I, quoth 'a! – at whose suit[16]? By my troth, yes, I'll
go: a cambric apron, gloves, a pair of purple stockings, and a
stomacher! I'll sweat in purple[17], mistress, for you; I'll take
anything that comes a' God's name[18]. O rich, a cambric apron!
Faith then, have at uptails all[19] – I'll go jiggy-joggy to London
and be here in a trice, young mistress. [*Exit Sybil.*]
ROSE Do so, good Sybil. Meantime wretched I
Will sit and sigh for his lost company.

[1]*Doctors' Commons* lodging-house for lawyers

[2]*out of cry* beyond all measure

[3]*Marry gup* My, aren't we getting above ourselves?

[4]*wanion* vengeance

[5]*humorous* moody

[6]*bushel* measure of eight gallons

[7]*stamped crabs* crab-apples crushed for their sour juice

[8]*verjuice* juice of unripe fruit, used in cooking

[9]*gaskins . . . netherstocks* breeches . . . stockings; i.e., though I may be outwardly civil to you, don't imagine we are intimate friends

[10]*go by, Jeronimo, go by* a hackneyed phrase meaning 'be off with you!'

[11]*driblets* petty debts

[12]*I'd . . . giblets* proverbial expressions, urging Rose to consider what she's letting herself in for

[13]*sigh* i.e., for a man

[14]*proper* handsome

[15]*snick up* hang

[16]*at whose suit?* need you ask?

[17]*sweat in purple* i.e., be damned for wearing rich clothes

[18]*a' God's name* free, for nothing

[19]*have . . . all* let's get a move on

MAGRIT	DOREEN
30s	19
Glasgow	Glasgow

The Steamie
Tony Roper

First presented by Wildcat Stage Productions at the Crawford Theatre, Jordanhill College of Education, Glasgow in 1987 and later at the Greenwich Theatre, London.

The play is set in a washhouse – the steamie – on a New Year's Eve in the late Fifties in Glasgow, where four women, old Mrs Culfeathers, her friend Dolly, Magrit and Doreen wash, scrub, have a few drinks and gossip their way through Hogmanay.

In this scene, Mrs Culfeathers has moved away to find a wringer for her enormous load of washing. Dolly goes to help her, leaving Magrit and Doreen on their own.

Published in *Scot-Free: New Scottish Plays* by Nick Hern Books, London

Act One

MAGRIT Christ there they go Saint Dolly and Blessed Molly Culfeathers.

DOREEN It's a shame but though i'n't it?

MAGRIT D y'e want a cigarette?

DOREEN Aye. Takin' in washing at her age.

[*Magrit searches in her coat for cigarettes.*]

What age wid she be?

MAGRIT I cannae find the bloody cigarettes noo. See if that wee swine Peter's taken them, I'll bloody murder him. Oh, here they are.

DOREEN Have ye caught him smokin'?

MAGRIT Naw no yit, but see if you go intae the lavy after him the place is reekin' and there's aye a wee dout in the pan, 'cause they'll no sink ye know. Ah aye know when he's been at it cause he keeps flushin' it tae try an' make it go away. Here, look at that, there was seven in there before I left ... there's only six noo.

DOREEN Ye should tell his faither.

MAGRIT I will ... the first time ah catch him sober. [*Lights cigarette.*] What were ye sayin' aboot Molly Culfeathers?

DOREEN She said she's been here since wan o'clock. Imagine havin' tae take in washin' at her age. Y'ed think her family wid help her oot.

MAGRIT Ah know. It's a disgrace, she'll no hear a word against them either.

DOREEN She must feel it herself though. Two sons she had?

MAGRIT Aye. Christ they wantit fur nothin' they two. Of course the old fellah had a good joab, ah don't know what he did, but he'd good money. Ah mind ma mother sayin' she'd aye a big bag o' messages every Saturday n'aw paid fur. Never ony tic. N'a lovely hoose tae. She's still goat a lovely hoose. Ma mother goes up noo'n'again. She says it's spotless, s'auld fashioned of course ... no oor taste.

DOREEN Ah think it's terrible, ah'd never treat mah mother like that, she charges one and six a washin'. I mean she's been here since wan o'clock, what is it noo? Efter seven ... that's say six hoors ... three washin's that's four and six, nae wonder the old soul's no celebratin' the New Year, she's goat nuthin tae celebrate, the auld fellah's no long fur this world either.

MAGRIT Oh when he goes, she'll no be long behind him.

DOREEN Aye, an' wait ye see the two hert broken sons at the funeral, they're in England aren't they?

MAGRIT Ah think so.

DOREEN John wantit us tae go tae England after we goat merrit, but ah didnae fancy it. I mean ye widnae know anybody. Would ye?

MAGRIT Right enough.

DOREEN I cannae stand the wey they talk aw yon ya ya ya.

MAGRIT Oh. They're a pain in the airse, see yon bloody British pictures.

DOREEN Ah know, they're loupin i'n't they?

MAGRIT We went tae the Rex aboot a week ago tae see ... eh whit wis it called eh Fred McMurray and eh ...

DOREEN 'Double Indemnity'.

MAGRIT It was great wint it?

DOREEN It was marvellous.

MAGRIT But did ye see thon thing that was oan wi' it?

DOREEN Aye, Ron Randell leanin' up against a lamp post smokin' a fag.

MAGRIT He tells ye the bloody story before ye've seen it.

DOREEN Aye'n'en he flicks the fag away, supposed tae be tough. 'N' says 'It was moorder'. They cannae fight right either, know how in the yankee pictures they belt wan another dead hard wi' their fists n'at see if there's a fight'n' the British wans, they wrestle aw the time.

MAGRIT So they dae, it's like an auld fashioned waltz.

DOREEN They never touch wan another. I mean in the yankee pictures they actually dae hit wan another. You can see them daen it.

MAGRIT Oh aye. Jimmy Cagney's a rerr wee fighter. Can ye imagine Jimmy Cagney in wan ae they British pictures. He'd murder the whole lot o' them.

DOREEN Aye. Nae bother. Have ye ever seen Tony Curtis?

MAGRIT Naw. Ah've heard ae him though.

DOREEN Oh he's beautiful.

MAGRIT Is he a fine boy?

DOREEN Oh whit . . . oh ye want tae see him. He's goat a fantastic haircut, and beautiful eyes 'n' a dead low voice, but his eyes though oh they go right in tae you. 'N' he wears smashin' clothes tae. John 'n' I went tae a picture he wis in. It was the first time ah'd seen him . . . I just sat there . . . I'm no kidding ye Magrit I was actually droolin', ma insides were aw going', see when the lights came up I didnae know where tae look. I was dead embarrassed . . . John says tae me 'Are you aw right ye're aw flushed. What's the matter?'

MAGRIT Whit d'ye say?

DOREEN I just telt him it was women's troubles, well so it was in a way.

MAGRIT Did he believe ye?

DOREEN Aye . . . he bought me an ice-cream tae help cool me doon. [*They laugh.*]

MAGRIT [*still laughing*] An did it?

DOREEN [*still laughing*] Naw. It was aw meltit by the time he goat back.

MAGRIT He should've goat ye an ice lolly . . . at least it would've been the right shape . . . oh ah've drapt ma fag . . . that's God punishin' me. Ah'm terrible so ah ahm sometimes.

DOREEN Will ye need tae tell that when ye go tae confess?

MAGRIT Naw. It would be too complicatit trying tae explain it aw tae the Priest, I'll stick in something else. That'll make up for it.

STEVIE   AUNT
50s   elderly

Stevie
Hugh Whitemore

First performed at the Vaudeville Theatre, London in 1977.

The play follows the life and career of poetess Stevie Smith, who lives with her elderly aunt in a small semi-detached house in North London. The time extends from the Fifties to the Sixties – up to Stevie's death at the age of 69.

In this opening scene, Aunt is watering the pot plants as Stevie enters, carrying her handbag and a plastic shopping-bag. She talks to her aunt and to the audience.

Published by Samuel French, London

Act One

STEVIE [*off*] I'm back! [*She slams the front door.*] I'm back! Where are you?

AUNT In here.

 [*Stevie enters.*]

 You're home nice and early.

STEVIE I'm utterly exhausted, worn to a frazzle. [*She puts her carrier-bag and handbag on the chaise, starts to take her coat off.*]

AUNT The kettle's on. I'll make a pot of tea.

STEVIE Is there anything to eat?

AUNT Battenburg cake and some ginger nuts.

STEVIE How lovely!

AUNT Give me your coat.

STEVIE Has anything happened today?

AUNT Nothing out of the ordinary.

 [*Aunt takes Stevie's coat, and exits.*]

STEVIE When I'm asked at the Day of Judgement what I remember best and what has ruled my whole life, I think I shall say: 'Being tired, too tired for words.'

[*Stevie sits at the desk chair and opens letters.*]

STEVIE I've been at the BBC, recording a story. I don't know why I bothered, it was a complete waste of time. The producer seemed to have quite a different idea about the story from mine. We got more and more at cross purposes, and a Mr Hall, who was sitting on the floor listening, said he couldn't make head or tail of it.

[*Aunt enters, carrying a plate of cake and ginger nuts.*]

AUNT Head or tail of what? [*She puts the plate on the coffee table.*]

STEVIE This is my aunt.

AUNT Who are you talking about?

STEVIE His name was Mr Hall.

AUNT Head or tail of *what*?

STEVIE A short story I'd written.

AUNT Poor man, I know how he felt. [*She looks for her glasses.*]

STEVIE I call her the 'Lion of Hull'. She looks very lion-like, don't you think?

[*Aunt is still searching amongst the books on the piano.*]

The dress is new, by the way. It reminds me of one of those seed packets, you know, Carter's Tested Seeds. I call it 'Every One Came Up'.

AUNT Where are my glasses, Peggy?

STEVIE In the fruit bowl.

AUNT All these books, just look at them!

STEVIE Not a literary person, thank God.

AUNT [*finding her glasses*] I've never seen so much stuff and nonsense in all my life.

[*Aunt exits.*]

STEVIE [*sitting on the chaise*] Stuff and nonsense are the twin bogies of my dear Aunt's existence, and she tilts against these pet windmills with all the courage of a latter-day Don Quixote. 'Stuff and Nonsense' is her call to arms, her battle-cry.

[*Aunt enters, carrying the tea-tray.*]

AUNT [*putting the tray on the pouffe*] That stupid kitchen tap needs a new washer. Tarnation take it.

[*Aunt goes to her chair.*]

Where's my cushion?

STEVIE Here, sorry.

[*Stevie takes the cushion from the chaise and gives it to Aunt.*]

AUNT You can never find anything in this house.

[*Aunt pours the tea.*]

STEVIE Smart writing people think it's not at all chic to live in the suburbs with an aunt, but I don't care what they think. I've never cared about chic things, fashion and so on. What does it matter? I love Aunt and Aunt loves me. That's what really matters.

AUNT Tea, dear?

STEVIE Thank you, darling.

[*Stevie takes a tea-cup from Aunt, who settles into her chair. Stevie sits on the chaise and sips tea.*]

AUNT Good?

STEVIE Mmm! Well now, where shall I begin?

AUNT Begin at the beginning and go through to the end, that's what I always say.

STEVIE Yes, and quite right too. Well. The twentieth of September, nineteen hundred and two: that was the beginning for me. The twentieth of September. Virgo. Rather a prim sign I always think, so I like to pretend I'm a bit of a Libra, too.

AUNT A Yorkshire lass, born in Hull. Thirty-four Delapole Avenue, such a nice house.

STEVIE We left when I was only three, so I don't remember much about it. Just wearing a pale blue coat, and having strawberries and cream on a vast stretch of bright green grass with people in white on it.

AUNT A Cricket Club tea.

STEVIE It must've been, yes. And so, on an autumn afternoon in nineteen hundred and six, my mother, my aunt, my five-year-old sister Molly and I arrived here in Palmers Green.

AUNT All those years ago! It doesn't seem possible.

STEVIE She was a romantic girl, my mama, and because of this she made what they call an 'unsuitable' marriage.

AUNT If your grandma had lived your mother and father would never have met, let alone married.

STEVIE And where would Stevie have been then, poor thing?

AUNT He was a great believer in independence, your grandfather. 'Decide for yourself,' he was always saying, and that's just what she did.

[*The front-door knocker bangs.*]

There's my paper.

[*Aunt exits.*]

STEVIE My mother was a romantic girl
So she had to marry a man with his hair in curl
Who subsequently became my unrespected papa,

115

But that was a long time ago now.
[*Aunt enters with the newspaper and sits reading.*]
What folly it is that daughters are always supposed to be
In love with papa. It wasn't the case with me.
I couldn't take to him at all
But he took to me
What a sad fate to befall
A child of three.

I sat upright in my baby carriage
And wished mama hadn't made such a foolish marriage.
I tried to hide it, but it showed in my eyes unfortunately
And a fortnight later papa ran away to sea.

He used to come home on leave
It was always the same
I could not grieve
But I think I am somewhat to blame.

AUNT Kent are doing badly: eighty-five for six.

STEVIE So with my father sailing the seven seas, we came here to Avondale Road. When we had settled ourselves in, we went round the corner to our landlord's shop, he was a plumber, a tall, thin man who looked like Charles the Second, we went round the corner to make some arrangements and to get me weighed.

AUNT You were always being weighed for one reason or another.

STEVIE He had some enormous weighing machines, I remember, the sort they use for luggage.

AUNT 'You're a fine package,' he said, lifting you onto the scales. 'I came on a train,' you said, 'on a train, and then on a tram.' And so you did, bless your heart.

STEVIE He was wrong, that plumber. I wasn't a fine package at all. I was always being ill.

AUNT That's why I came to London. Someone had to look after you, with your mother being so weak and poorly.

STEVIE Yes, I often wish I'd been a bright, healthy child, but I wasn't and that's that. Fate, I suppose. Stevie's fate.

AUNT Fate, indeed!

STEVIE I believe in fate, I really do.

MOZART
young

CONSTANZE
young

Amadeus
Peter Shaffer

First performed at the National Theatre in 1977 and later transferred to Her Majesty's Theatre, London.

The action takes place in Vienna in the year 1823 and flashes back to the period between 1781 and 1791 as Antonio Salieri, now an old man near to death, looks back on his brilliant career as Court Composer. He recalls his hatred of the young genius, Mozart, whose music he could never equal, and step by step recounts how he brought about his financial ruin and eventual demise. Now Mozart is poor and almost starving, complaining of stomach cramps and 'seeing' a tall grey figure materialising in front of him.

In this scene, set in his apartment, he is writing music with a blanket around his shoulders, while his heavily pregnant young wife, Constanze, sits opposite him wrapped in her shawl.

Published by Penguin Plays, London

Act Two

CONSTANZE I'm cold ... I'm cold all day ... Hardly surprising since we have no firewood.

MOZART Papa was right. We end exactly as he said. Beggars.

CONSTANZE It's all his fault.

MOZART What do you mean?

CONSTANZE He kept you a baby all your life.

MOZART I don't understand ... You always loved Papa.

CONSTANZE *I* did?

MOZART You adored him. You told me so often.

[*Slight pause.*]

CONSTANZE [*flatly*] I hated him.

MOZART What?

CONSTANZE And he hated me.

117

MOZART That's absurd. He loved us both very much. You're being extremely silly now.

CONSTANZE Am I?

MOZART [*airily*] Yes, you are, little-wife-of-my-heart!

CONSTANZE Do you remember the fire we had last night, because it was so cold you couldn't even get the ink wet? You said 'What a blaze' – remember? 'What a blaze! All those old papers going up!' Well, my dear, those old papers were just all your father's letters, that's all – every one he wrote since the day we married.

MOZART *What?*

CONSTANZE Every one! All the letters about what a ninny I am – what a bad housekeeper I am! Every one!

MOZART [*crying out*] Stanzi!

CONSTANZE *Shit on him! ... Shit on him!*

MOZART *You bitch!*

CONSTANZE [*savagely*] At least it kept us warm! What else will do that? Perhaps we should dance! You love to dance, Wolferl – let's dance! Dance to keep warm! [*grandly*] Write me a contredanze, Mozart! It's your job to write dances, isn't it?
[*Hysterical, she starts dancing roughly round the room like a demented peasant to the tune of 'Non più andrai'.*]
[*singing wildly*] *Non più andrai, farfallone amoroso –*
Notte e giorno d'intorno girando!

MOZART [*shrieking*] *Stop it! Stop it!* [*He seizes her.*] Stanzi-marini! Marini-bini! Don't please! Please, please, please I beg you ... Look there's a kiss! Where's it coming from? Right out of that corner! There's another one – all wet, all sloppy wet coming straight to *you.* Kiss – kiss – kiss!
[*She pushes him away. Constanze dances. Mozart catches her. She pushes him away.*]

CONSTANZE Get off!
[*Pause.*]

MOZART I'm frightened, Stanzi. Something awful's happening to me.

CONSTANZE I can't bear it. I can't bear much more of this.

MOZART And the Figure's like this now – [*beckoning faster*] 'Here! Come here! Here!' Its face still masked – invisible! It becomes realer and realer to me!

CONSTANZE Stop it, for God's sake! ... Stop! ... It's me who's frightened ... *Me!* ... You frighten me ... If you go on like this I'll leave you. I swear it.

MOZART [*shocked*] Stanzi!

CONSTANZE I mean it ... I do ... [*She puts her hand to her stomach, as if in pain.*]

MOZART I'm sorry ... Oh God, I'm sorry ... I'm sorry, I'm sorry, I'm sorry! ... Come here to me, little wife of my heart! Come ... Come ...
[*He kneels and coaxes her to him. She comes half-reluctantly, half-willingly.*]

MOZART Who am I? ... Quick: tell me. Hold me and tell who I am.

CONSTANZE Pussy-wussy.

MOZART Who else?

CONSTANZE Miaowy-powy.

MOZART And you're squeeky-peeky. And Stanzi-manzi. And Binigini!
[*She surrenders.*]

CONSTANZE Wolfi-polfi!

MOZART Poopy-peepee!
[*They giggle.*]

CONSTANZE Now don't be stupid.

MOZART [*insistent: like a child*] Come on – do it. Do it – Let's do it. Poppy!
[*They play a private game, gradually doing it faster, on their knees.*]

CONSTANZE Poppy.

MOZART [*changing it*] Pappy.

CONSTANZE [*copying*] Pappy.

MOZART Pappa.

CONSTANZE Pappa.

MOZART Pappa-pappa!

CONSTANZE Pappa-pappa!

MOZART Pappa-pappa-pappa-pappa!

CONSTANZE Pappa-pappa-pappa-pappa!
[*They rub noses.*]

TOGETHER Pappa-pappa-pappa-pappa! Pappa-pappa-pappa-pappa!

CONSTANZE *Ah!*
[*She suddenly cries out in distress, and clutches her stomach.*]

MOZART Stanzi! ... Stanzi, what is it?

ELIOT GREEN   LESLEY GREEN
13   young

Bar Mitzvah Boy
Jack Rosenthal

First shown on television in 1976, and set in Willesden, North
London.

The action revolves around young Eliot Green who, trau-
matised by his family's elaborate arrangements for his bar
mitzvah, finally walks out in the middle of the ceremony. Eliot
has completely disappeared and the family are distraught, all
their plans for the great day in ruins.

In this scene Eliot is sitting in the middle of a children's
playground. His elder sister, Lesley, enters, looking for him.
As soon as he spots her he puts on a Mickey Mouse mask.
Lesley sees him, strolls over unhurriedly and sits down next
to him.

Published by Penguin Plays, London

Scene Sixty-six

LESLEY I should always wear it. It's a hell of an improvement.
  [*He at once takes it off.*
  They sit watching the children.]
  Having a terrific time, are you? We've had a terrific time. We went
  to the synagogue. It was a good laugh. Pity you couldn't stay.
  [*Eliot seems to have decided never to speak again. He sits
  watching the children.*]
  Listen, Nutcase. There are two alternatives. Either we talk, or
  I smash your face in. It's entirely up to you. [*No reply.*] In a
  minute, there'll be *one* alternative.
ELIOT Are they upset?
LESLEY 'Upset'?
ELIOT Are they?
LESLEY Oh, brilliant! No, they're having bloody sing-song! Eliot
  – for God's sake – the most important day of their lives!

[*A pause.*]
Well?
[*Eliot shrugs. Then sighs.*]
ELIOT I went for a haircut by the way.
LESLEY You what??
ELIOT I didn't have one though.
LESLEY You went for a *bar mitzvah* ... you didn't have one of those either! What the hell do you mean you went for a haircut! Is that why you left? To go for a sodding haircut?
ELIOT 'Course not.
LESLEY Well, why?
[*A pause.*]
Why, Eliot?
ELIOT I don't think I'm old enough to be bar mitzvah'd.
[*Lesley stares at him, completely nonplussed.*]
LESLEY You're thirteen. That's the *age*.
ELIOT I don't think I've got the qualifications.
LESLEY *What* qualifications? The only qualification is to be thirteen! All you've to do is breathe for thirteen years and avoid the *traffic*! What the hell are you talking about?
[*A pause.*
A ball rolls towards them, accidentally thrown there by a couple of kids playing. Eliot picks it up and throws it back to them.]
ELIOT I don't think I believe in them, Lesley.
LESLEY In what?
ELIOT Bar mitzvahs. I don't think they work.
LESLEY [*confused, exasperated*] Eliot. Every Jewish boy gets bar mitzvah'd. Every single one. For thousands of years!
ELIOT [*helpfully*] Five thousand seven hundred and thirty six.
LESLEY [*accepting his help*] Five thousand seven hundred and thirty six. Everybody. Dad did it. Grandad. Harold ...
ELIOT They're not men, Lesley.
[*The simple sentence is like a terrible smack across the face. Calm now, very grave, very concerned, Lesley stares at him.*]
That's the whole point. If that's being a man, I don't want to be one, do I? And it was no good pretending I did.
[*A pause.*
Lesley is beginning to understand the truth of what he's said. It hurts her and saddens her.]
LESLEY [*lamely*] What are they then? If they're not men? Giraffes?

[*A pause.*

The ball comes rolling towards them again from the two chil-dren playing. They're both too preoccupied to return it.]

[FIRST KID (*calling*) Can we have our ball back, missus? (*Pause.*) Oy! Grandma! Cloth-ears!]

[*Lesley, absently, throws it back to them.*]

LESLEY [*apprehensive about what Eliot may reply*] Dad's a man, Eliot . . .

ELIOT [*calmly, reasonably; he's thought it all out many times before*] If he was my age and behaved like he does, he'd get a clip round the ear. Dad's a big spoilt kid, Lesley. Do you know why I wouldn't go for a haircut yesterday? Because everybody wanted me to. I was being a stupid kid. Awkward. Like dad. He doesn't care tuppence what other people want. That's ignorant, really, in a grown man.

[*A pause.*]

LESLEY [*even more apprehensively*] And Harold?

ELIOT Harold does everything that everybody wants. That's even worse. He's scared *not* to. He's scared all the time. *You* ought to know. [*Pause.*] Grandad wants everybody to think the world of him just because he's Grandad. Just because he's there. Like babies do. Little babies in prams.

[*A pause.*

Lesley knows it's all true. The more certain she is, the angrier she feels towards Eliot: she wants to lash out wildly.]

LESLEY And that's what you think, is it?

ELIOT [*sadly*] Rotten, isn't it? It makes my chest hurt.

LESLEY It's your considered opinion?

ELIOT I'm not saying they're the only ones. That's the trouble. It's every feller you . . .

LESLEY Well, here's *my* considered opinion, Eliot. You're a bloody liar! It's all an excuse, you lying sod! You ran away because you couldn't do it! Because you were frightened you'd forgotten what you'd learnt!

ELIOT I wasn't, Lesley.

LESLEY You thought you'd get it all wrong! That you'd make a nudnik of yourself! You were chicken!

ELIOT [*wearily*] Lesley, I could do it standing on my head.

LESLEY Go on, then! Prove it!

ELIOT Look, all I'm saying is . . .

LESLEY I know what you're saying! That all the men you've ever known . . . and your own dad, and Grandad, and Harold . . .

all did what you couldn't! What you weren't even man enough
to *try*!

ELIOT They did ... but they *didn't* ... [*With growing frustration.*]
... they didn't mean what they ...

LESLEY They *tried*! They're *still* bloody trying for all you know!
You didn't! And they're the babies? You're a liar, Eliot. The
whole thing's an excuse. You're a bloody liar.

[*A pause.*]

ELIOT [*almost to himself*] I could do it standing on my head ...

[*A pause.*

*Lesley watches the kids playing, then, as though she considers
the discussion over, she gets up and starts brushing grass from
her clothes, apparently ready to leave.*

*Eliot sits staring ahead at the children playing. After a moment
or two, he gets to his feet, puts his hands on the ground and
levers himself up so that he's standing on his head. He begins
to recite the first Hebrew blessing of his bar mitzvah.*

Lesley stares at him, blankly.]

JOHN PROCTOR
30s

ELIZABETH PROCTOR
30s

The Crucible
Arthur Miller

First presented in England at the Bristol Old Vic in 1954 and set in Salem, Massachussetts.

The play is based on the witch-hunt of 1692, where a small community is stirred into madness and innocent people are 'cried out' as witches and hanged. John Proctor, a well-respected farmer, has allowed himself to be seduced by the wiles of his 17-year-old servant, Abigail Williams. His wife, Elizabeth, has dismissed the girl, and now Abigail has accused her of witchcraft.

In this scene, Elizabeth, realising that Abigail wants her dead so that she can take her place, insists that John makes a final break with her so that she no longer has a hold over him.

Published by Penguin Plays, London

Act Two

ELIZABETH [*quietly*] Oh, the noose, the noose is up!

PROCTOR There'll be no noose.

ELIZABETH She wants me dead. I knew all week it would come to this!

PROCTOR [*without conviction*] They dismissed it. You heard her say—

ELIZABETH And what of tomorrow? She will cry me out until they take me!

PROCTOR Sit you down.

ELIZABETH She wants me dead, John, you know it!

PROCTOR I say sit down! [*She sits, trembling. He speaks quietly, trying to keep his wits.*] Now we must be wise, Elizabeth.

ELIZABETH [*with sarcasm, and a sense of being lost*] Oh, indeed, indeed!

PROCTOR Fear nothing. I'll find Ezekiel Cheever. I'll tell him she said it were all sport.

ELIZABETH John, with so many in the jail, more than Cheever's help is needed now, I think. Would you favour me with this? Go to Abigail.

PROCTOR [*his soul hardening as he senses ...*] What have I to say to Abigail?

ELIZABETH [*delicately*] John – grant me this. You have a faulty understanding of young girls. There is a promise made in any bed—

PROCTOR [*striving against his anger*] What promise?

ELIZABETH Spoke or silent, a promise is surely made. And she may dote on it now – I am sure she does – and thinks to kill me, then to take my place.

[*Proctor's anger is rising; he cannot speak.*]

ELIZABETH It is her dearest hope, John, I know it. There be a thousand names; why does she call mine? There be a certain danger in calling such a name – I am no Goody Good that sleeps in ditches, nor Osburn, drunk and half-witted. She'd dare not call out such a farmer's wife but there be monstrous profit in it. She thinks to take my place, John.

PROCTOR She cannot think it! [*He knows it is true.*]

ELIZABETH [*reasonably*] John, have you ever shown her somewhat of contempt? She cannot pass you in the church but you will blush—

PROCTOR I may blush for my sin.

ELIZABETH I think she sees another meaning in that blush.

PROCTOR And what see you? What see you, Elizabeth?

ELIZABETH [*conceding*] I think you be somewhat ashamed, for I am there, and she so close.

PROCTOR When will you know me, woman? Were I stone I would have cracked for shame this seven month!

ELIZABETH Then go and tell her she's a whore. Whatever promise she may sense – break it, John, break it.

PROCTOR [*between his teeth*] Good, then. I'll go. [*He starts for his rifle.*]

ELIZABETH [*trembling, fearfully*] Oh, how unwillingly!

PROCTOR [*turning on her, rifle in hand*] I will curse her hotter than the oldest cinder in hell. But pray, begrudge me not my anger!

ELIZABETH Your anger! I only ask you—

PROCTOR Woman, am I so base? Do you truly think me base?

ELIZABETH I never called you base.

PROCTOR Then how do you charge me with such a promise? The promise that a stallion gives a mare I gave that girl!

ELIZABETH Then why do you anger with me when I bid you break it?

PROCTOR Because it speaks deceit, and I am honest! But I'll plead no more! I see now your spirit twists around the single error of my life, and I will never tear it free!

ELIZABETH [*crying out*] You'll tear it free – when you come to know that I will be your only wife, or no wife at all! She has an arrow in you yet, John Proctor, and you know it well!

COCKLEBURY-SMYTHE
young/middle-aged

MADDIE GOTOBED
young

Dirty Linen and New-Found-Land
Tom Stoppard

The first performance was at Inter-Action's tiny Almost Free Theatre in Rupert Street in 1976 and the play transferred later to the Arts Theatre, London.

Dirty Linen concerns the investigations of a Select Committee into moral standards in the House of Commons, where it is rumoured that 'a sexual swathe' has passed through Westminster claiming the reputations of no fewer than 119 members. The phrase 'Mystery Woman' is being bandied about in the press and there is no doubt that 'someone is going through the ranks like a lawn-mower in knickers'.

In this scene, Cocklebury-Smythe, a sharp, smooth-talking MP, is persuading Maddie Gotobed, the sexy, obliging young secretary seconded to the Committee from the Home Office typing pool, to 'forget' about their recent 'liaisons' at Crockford's, Claridges and the Coq d'Or. Cocklebury-Smythe's first speech is interrupted by McTeazle, another MP, who looks in briefly to retrieve his hat. He returns later and takes over the scene from Cocklebury-Smythe. The words in italics coincide with McTeazle's appearances.

Published by Faber & Faber, London

COCKLEBURY-SMYTHE Maddie my dear, you look even more ravishing this morning than *the smallest specified number of members of that committee of which* we will have to be very very careful – it is a cruel irony that our carefree little friend-ship, which is as innocent and pure as the first driven snow-drop of spring, is in danger of being trampled by the hobnailed hue-and-cry over these absurd rumours of unbuttoned behav-iour in and out of both trousers of Parliament – I think I can say, and say with confidence, that when the smoke has cleared from the Augean stables, the little flame of our love will still be something no one else can hold a candle to so long as we can keep our heads down. In other words, my darling girl, if anyone were to ask you where you had lunch on Friday, breakfast on Saturday or dinner on Sunday, best thing is to forget Crockford's, Claridges and the Coq d'Or.

MADDIE [*concentrating*] Crockford's – Claridges – the Coq d'Or.

COCKLEBURY-SMYTHE Forget – forget.

MADDIE Forget. Forget Crockford's, Claridges, Coq d'Or. Forget Crockford's, Claridges, Coq d'Or. [*To herself.*] Forget Crockford's, Claridges, Coq d'Or. Forget Crockford's, Claridges, Coq d'Or.

[*Cocklebury-Smythe sees that this is achieving the opposite.*]

COCKLEBURY-SMYTHE All right – tell you what – say you had *breakfast* at Claridges, *lunch* at the Coq d'Or, and had *dinner* at Crockford's. Meanwhile I'll stick to—

MADDIE [*concentrating harder than ever*] Claridges, Coq d'Or, Crockford's. Forget Crockford's, Claridges, Coq d'Or. Remember Claridges, Coq d'Or, Crockford's. Remember Claridges, Coq d'Or, Crockford's. Claridges, Coq d'Or, Crockford's, Claridges, Coq d'Or, Crockford's.

COCKLEBURY-SMYTHE But not with me.

MADDIE Not with you. Not with Cockie at Claridges, Coq d'Or, Crockford's. Never at Claridges, Coq d'Or, Crockford's with Cockie. Never at Claridges, Coq d'Or, Crockford's with Cockie.

[*Her concentration doesn't imply slowness: she is fast, eager, breathless, very good at tongue twisters. Her whole attitude in the play is one of innocent, eager willingness to please. Cocklebury-Smythe sees that he is going about this the wrong way.*]

COCKLEBURY-SMYTHE Wait a minute. [*Rapidly.*] The best thing is forget Claridges, Crockford's and the Coq d'Or altogether.

MADDIE Right. Forget Claridges, Crockford's, Coq d'Or – forget Claridges, Crockford's, Coq d'Or—

COCKLEBURY-SMYTHE And if anyone asks you where you had lunch on Friday, breakfast on Saturday and dinner last night, when you were with me, tell them where you had dinner on Friday, lunch on Saturday and breakfast yesterday.

MADDIE Right! [*Pause. She closes her eyes with concentration.*] [*Rapidly.*] The Green Cockatoo, the Crooked Clock, the Crock of Gold – and Box Hill.

COCKLEBURY-SMYTHE Box Hill?

MADDIE To see the moon come up – forget Crockford's, Claridges, Coq d'Or – remember the Crock of Gold, Box Hill, the Crooked Clock and the Green Door—

COCKLEBURY-SMYTHE Cockatoo—

MADDIE Cockatoo. Crock of Gold, Crooked Clock, Green Cockatoo and Box Hill. When was this?

COCKLEBURY-SMYTHE When you were really with me.

MADDIE Right. With Cockie at the Green Cockatoo—

COCKLEBURY-SMYTHE No *not* with Cockie at the Green Cockatoo.

MADDIE —not with Cockie at the Green Cockatoo, the Old Cook, the Crooked Grin, Gamages and Box Hill.

COCKLEBURY-SMYTHE [*wildly*] No – look. The simplest thing is to forget, Claridges, the Old Boot, the Golden *quorum can be any number agreed upon by—*
[*This is because McTeazle is back.*]

[MCTEAZLE Douglas is on his way back. (*Hanging up his hat.*)]

COCKLEBURY-SMYTHE I've got to have a drink.

RACHEL
late 40s
Jamaican

STONE
45
Jamaican

An Echo in the Bone
Dennis Scott

First presented by the University Drama Society at the Creative Arts Centre, Jamaica in 1974.

The play is set during a traditional Nine Night Ceremony to honour the spirit of the dead. Rachel's husband, Crew, has gone missing and is presumed dead. Rachel has invited his friends and neighbours to the Wake. All the characters are black and throughout the ceremony they act out scenes from past and present.

Crew is thought to have murdered Mister Charles, the white Estate owner. In this scene Stone acts out Mister Charles, who three years previously seduced Rachel, and who has come back to offer her a job as his housekeeper.

Published in *Plays for Today* by Longman, London

Act Two

STONE [*off, singing softly*] 'Moonshine tonight,' [*He is at the door. Rachel is frozen with her back to him.*] Good afternoon. Rachel. [*She turns slowly.*] May I come in? [*Silence.*] And sit down? It's a long walk over the back meadow, but I wasn't sure I wanted to see anybody on my way. [*Sits.*] Still a fine woman ...

RACHEL Mass Charlie.

STONE How many years now, Rachel? [*Pause.*]

RACHEL Three, Mass Charlie.

STONE Respectful as ever. Is anybody here? [*Shakes her head.*] That's a fine boy you have. Three years? How they grow.

RACHEL Not a boy anymore, Sir.

STONE Jack, wasn't it?

RACHEL Isaac, we call him Sonson.

STONE Ah yes, could I bother you for a drink? [*She moves to get it.*] Insolent though. You must be proud of him, has your spirit.

130

RACHEL [*levelly*] Is his father in him, Master Charles. (*Pours.*)

STONE Yes, I remember there are two. [*Takes the glass.*] Thank you. Ah, country tastes. The best, always. I have missed this place.

RACHEL My husband is not here now, sir. I can direct you to the acreage if you want.

STONE Sit down, Rachel.

RACHEL You want him to come up to the Great House tomorrow and see you?

STONE Sit down. [*She sits.*] How have you been, Rachel?

RACHEL Things are the same as ever.

[*He takes it at face value.*]

STONE From I was a boy, I found it strange that things changed so slowly here, or not at all. Tell me how things are, Rachel.

RACHEL Mister Charles—

STONE I want to know. [*Silence.*]

RACHEL The farm is doing well.

STONE Have you roofed the house yet?

RACHEL Last April.

STONE In time for the rains.

RACHEL But it was a dry season.

STONE I heard. [*Silence.*]

RACHEL What you want, Mr Charles?

STONE I have come home, Rachel.

RACHEL You staying long, Mr Charles?

STONE For good. I've come back to my people. [*Rachel laughs. After a moment he laughs too.*] Nice and sour. [*She takes the glass.*]

RACHEL What you want, Mr Charles?

STONE I'd like to talk business for a while. [*Goes to the window.*] [*Stone moves back, she smiles.*]

STONE The old house is falling to ruin. It's a disgrace. Built well, mind you. Your ancestors worked hard at it. I'm sorry. I say the wrong things to you without meaning to. It's a fact, you know.

RACHEL It don't have nothing to do with me, Mr Charles.

STONE Now that I'll be here all year round, I'm going to find a staff for the place. Reliable people I can depend on. I need a good house keeper to start with. The job is yours.

RACHEL I have a family, Mr Charles.

STONE You'll have a staff of about four, I think, it's a big old house, though I'll probably close down half of it. Maybe make it into a museum. There's some fine stuff there from the past. My wife never appreciated it. Solid stuff. Enduring.

RACHEL Thank you for the offer, Sir. I will ask around in the village if you want.

STONE Ask around, hell! I know what I want. Of course it will take a while to change the place into the kind of house it should be. But there's no reason to wait, I need some good home cooking right now to fatten me up. I'd forgotten how much I missed it.

RACHEL I have a husband and two sons, Mr Charles. And one of them marrying soon. The house to keep and clothes to mend and food to prepare. That is a big enough job for one woman. You will have to find somebody responsible from town, a single woman.

STONE The pay is good. And you wouldn't have to sleep in except once or twice a week, perhaps, when I happen to have guests. You can do a lot to help your family, it's a responsible job, Rachel. The whole district will look up to you.

RACHEL Is so?

STONE You understand the job I'm offering you, Rachel?

RACHEL Yes.

STONE It's cold in England, Rachel. And with my wife dead, I was lonely. Did you like her?

RACHEL It wasn't my place to like or not to like.

STONE But you saw her with me sometimes. You could tell from the mouth alone, couldn't you. She was an ugly woman. But you get used to people.

RACHEL How you speak ill of the dead like that?

STONE I'm trying to tell you, I would have stayed away out of sheer habit if they could have stopped the cancer. But I kept seeing your face on every frosted window in London after she died. Calling me home. Different from winter. Different from white. Warmer than snow.

RACHEL How you can talk this way!

STONE Rachel, it's not as if we were strangers! We grew up here in the village, remember, long before you came to the back of the great house selling corn. We're part of this place, I can talk to you. You know that! If it's not true, what was it that make you so weak three years ago? So eager?

RACHEL You is a dirty, dirty man.

STONE Eh? Don't be so goddamn innocent! Are you ashamed, now? Where the hell do you get this sudden virtue from?

RACHEL I didn't know what I was doing, so help me God.

STONE You didn't know what you was doing! [*Laughs raucously.*]

RACHEL I was feeling so sorry for you, with that white bitch of a wife, that the whole district did know bout.

STONE Try again. Married how many, twenty years? And a great sorrow and sympathy takes hold of you, right in the middle of the stable, with the horses watching us steeplechase for a whole hour. Confess the truth, wasn't it the thought of the white man that made your skirt so easy to lift up? Eh, Rachel? Didn't you feel proud that you'd caught the richest man around here in between your legs?

RACHEL [*She moves to the window.*] You finish?

STONE You country slut. Oh, you had a good time that afternoon. And the next week too. One might have been an accident, but two! You remember what you said, eh? Lawd, it big! I did think is only black man make so!

FLORA CREWE
30s

NIRAD DAS
34
Indian

Indian Ink
Tom Stoppard

First performed at the Yvonne Arnaud Theatre, Guildford and transferred to the Aldwych Theatre, London in February 1995.

The play is set in two periods – 1930 (in India) and the mid-Eighties (in India and England) – and takes place against the background of the emergence of the Indian subcontinent from the grip of the Empire.

Flora Crewe is a young poet who has come to India in the Thirties as her doctor has advised a warmer climate. She meets Nirad Das, a local artist who asks if she would like to sit for a portrait. Fifty years later, the artist's son visits Flora's sister in London, while at the same time her would-be biographer continues his research in India.

In this early scene Flora has her first sitting with Das. They are on the verandah of her 'dak bungalow' in Jummapur. Flora sits writing in her notebook, while Das is painting. Her feet are bare and her shoes are placed neatly to one side. She pauses, thinking, sitting quite still.

Published by Faber & Faber, London

Act One
FLORA [*recorded*] 'Yes I am in heat like a bride in a bath,
   without secrets, soaked in heated air
   that liquifies to the touch and floods,
   shortening the breath, yes
   I am discovered, heat has found me out,
   a stain that stops at nothing,
   not the squeezed gates or soft gutters,
   it slicks into the press
   that prints me to the sheet
   yes, think of a woman in a house of net

that strains the oxygen out of the air
thickening the night to Indian ink
or think if you prefer—'
[*Flora has unconsciously crossed her legs, which brings Das's
work to a halt. He waits, patiently.*
She notices that Das has stopped.]
Oh . . .
DAS No, please be comfortable.
FLORA I'm sorry! [*She puts her feet side-by-side.*] There. Is that
how I was?
DAS You are patient with me. I think your nature is very kind.
FLORA Do you think so, Mr Das?
DAS I am sure of it. May I ask you a personal question?
FLORA That *is* a personal question.
DAS Oh my goodness, is it?
FLORA I always think so. It always feels like one. Carte blanche
is what you're asking, Mr Das. Am I to lay myself bare before
you?
DAS [*panicking slightly*] My question was only about your poem!
FLORA At least you knew it was personal.
DAS I will not ask it now, of course.
FLORA On that understanding I will answer it. My poem is about
heat.
DAS Oh. Thank you.
FLORA I resume my pose. Pen to paper. Legs uncrossed. You
know, you are the first man to paint my toe-nails.
DAS Actually, I am occupied in the folds of your skirt.
FLORA Ah. In that you are not the first.
DAS You have been painted before? – but of course you have!
Many times, I expect!
FLORA You know, Mr Das, your nature is much kinder than mine.
[*Flora resumes. Das resumes.*
*Anish Das comes into the Shepperton garden. He has a soft
briefcase; he sits in one of the garden chairs.*]
Mr Das, I have been considering whether to ask you a delicate
question, as between friends and artists.
DAS Oh, Miss Crewe, I am transported beyond my most fantastical
hopes of our fellowship! This is a red-letter day without dispute!
FLORA If you are going to be so Indian I shan't ask it.
DAS But I cannot be less Indian than I am.
FLORA You could if you tried. I'm not sure I'm going to ask you
now.

DAS Then you need not, dear Miss Crewe! You considered. The unasked, the almost asked question, united us for a moment in its intimacy, we came together in your mind like a spark in a vacuum glass, and the redness of the day's letter will not be denied.

FLORA You are still doing it, Mr Das.

DAS You wish me to be less Indian?

FLORA I did say that but I think what I meant was for you to be *more* Indian, or at any rate *Indian*, not Englished-up and all over me like a labrador and knocking things off tables with your tail – so *waggish* of you, Mr Das, to compare my mind to a vacuum. You only do it with us, I don't believe that left to yourself you can't have an ordinary conversation without jumping backwards through hoops of delight, *with* whoops of delight, I think I mean; actually, I do know what I mean, I want you to be with me as you would be if *I* were Indian.

DAS An Indian Miss Crewe! Oh dear, that is a mental construction which has no counterpart in the material world.

FLORA So is a *unicorn*, but you can imagine it.

DAS You can imagine it but you cannot mount it.

FLORA Imagining it was all I was asking in my case.

DAS [*terribly discomfited*] Oh! Oh, my gracious! – I had no intention – I assure you—

FLORA [*amused*] No, no, you cannot unwag your very best wag. You cleared the table, the bric-a-brac is on the Wilton – the specimen vase, the snuff box, the souvenir of Broadstairs— [*But she has misjudged.*]

DAS [*anguished*] You are cruel to me, Miss Crewe!

FLORA [*instantly repentant*] Oh! I'm so sorry. I didn't want to be. It's my nature. Please come out from behind your easel – look at me.

DAS May we fall silent, please. I prefer to work in silence.

FLORA I've spoiled everything. I'm very sorry.

DAS The shadow has moved. I must correct it.

FLORA Yes, it has moved. It cannot be corrected. We must wait for tomorrow. I'm so sorry.

BEN   MISS PRUE
young   young
seafaring accent

Love for Love
William Congreve

This Restoration comedy was first performed in 1695 by His
Majesty's Servants at the Theatre in Little Lincolns-Inn Fields
and is set in London.

Ben is a sailor and Sir Sampson's younger son – described
as 'a little rough' and in need of 'a little polish'. He has just
returned from a long sea voyage and his father is anxious for
him to marry and settle down.

In this scene Ben attempts to propose to Miss Prue, the young
daughter of his father's friend, old Foresight. However, she is
already in love with Tattle and wants nothing to do with him.

Published by A&C Black, London

Act Three, Scene Seven

BEN Come mistress, will you please to sit down, for an you stand
astern a that'n[1], we shall never grapple together. Come, I'll
haul a chair; there, an you please to sit, I'll sit by you.

MISS PRUE You need not sit so near one; if you have anything to
say, I can hear you farther off, I an't deaf.

BEN Why, that's true, as you say, nor I an't dumb; I can be heard
as far as another. I'll heave off to please you. [*Sits farther off.*]
An we were a league asunder, I'd undertake to hold discourse
with you, an 'twere not a main high wind indeed, and full in
my teeth. Look you forsooth, I am, as it were, bound for the
land of matrimony; 'tis a voyage, d'ye see, that was none of
my seeking. I was commanded by father, and if you like of it,
mayhap I may steer into your harbour. How say you, mistress?
The short of the thing is this, that if you like me, and I like
you, we may chance to swing in a hammock together.

MISS PRUE I don't know what to say to you, nor I don't care to
speak with you at all.

BEN No, I'm sorry for that. But pray, why are you so scornful?

MISS PRUE As long as one must not speak one's mind, one had better not speak at all, I think, and truly I won't tell a lie for the matter.

BEN Nay, you say true in that; it's but a folly to lie: for to speak one thing and to think just the contrary way is, as it were, to look one way, and to row another. Now, for my part, d'ye see, I'm for carrying things above board, I'm not for keeping anything under hatches; so that if you ben't as willing as I, say so, a God's name, there's no harm done; mayhap you may be shamefaced; some maidens, tho'f they love a man well enough, yet they don't care to tell'n so to's face. If that's the case, why, silence gives consent.

MISS PRUE But I'm sure it is not so, for I'll speak sooner than you should believe that; and I'll speak truth, though one should always tell a lie to a man; and I don't care, let my father do what he will; I'm too big to be whipped, so I'll tell you plainly, I don't like you, nor love you at all, nor never will, that's more. So there's your answer for you, and don't trouble me no more, you ugly thing.

BEN Look you, young woman, you may learn to give good words, however. I spoke you fair, d'ye see, and civil. As for your love or your liking, I don't value it of a rope's end; and mayhap I like you as little as you do me: what I said was in obedience to father; gad, I fear a whipping no more than you do. But I tell you one thing, if you should give such language at sea, you'd have a cat-o'-nine-tails laid cross your shoulders. Flesh! who are you? You heard t'other handsome young woman speak civilly to me of her own accord. Whatever you think of yourself, gad, I don't think you are any more to compare to her, than a can of small beer to a bowl of punch.

MISS PRUE Well, and there's a handsome gentleman, and a fine gentleman, and a sweet gentleman, that was here that loves me, and I love him; and if he sees you speak to me any more, he'll thrash your jacket for you, he will, you great sea-calf.

BEN What, do you mean that fair-weather spark that was here just now? Will he thrash my jacket? Let'n – let'n. But an he comes near me, mayhap I may giv'n a salt eel[2] for's supper, for all that. What does father mean to leave me alone as soon as I come home with such a dirty dowdy? Sea-calf? I an't calf enough to lick your chalked face, you cheese-curd you. Marry

thee! Ouns, I'll marry a Lapland witch as soon, and live upon
selling of contrary winds and wrecked vessels.

MISS PRUE I won't be called names, nor I won't be abused thus,
so I won't. If I were a man, [*cries*] you durst not talk at this
rate. No, you durst not, you stinking tar-barrel.

---

[1]*astern a that'n* she has turned her   [2]*salt eel* rope's end (a thrashing)
back on him

ISABELLA
young

CLAUDIO
young

Measure for Measure
William Shakespeare

First performed in 1604 and known as one of Shakespeare's 'dark comedies', the play is set in Vienna.

The Duke of Vienna, concerned about increasing immorality amongst his younger subjects, authorises his deputy, Lord Angelo, to enforce the long-disregarded laws against unchaste behaviour. Claudio is the first to be arrested for the crime of lechery and is condemned to death for the seduction of Juliet, a young girl whom he is about to marry and who is heavily pregnant by him. Unable to appeal to the Duke, who is supposedly away in Poland, Claudio sends his sister, Isabella, a novice nun, to plead with Angelo on his behalf. At first Angelo refuses to listen to Isabella, but then tells her to come back and see him again the next day. When she returns he says he will pardon her brother on condition that she will yield her body to him.

In this scene Isabella goes to the prison to tell Claudio he must prepare himself for death.

Act Three, Scene One

CLAUDIO Now, sister, what's the comfort?

ISABELLA Why,
    As all comforts are; most good, most good, indeed.
    Lord Angelo, having affairs to heaven,
    Intends you for his swift ambassador,
    Where you shall be an everlasting leiger.
    Therefore, your best appointment make with speed;
    To-morrow you set on.

CLAUDIO Is there no remedy?

ISABELLA None, but such remedy as, to save a head,
    To cleave a heart in twain.

CLAUDIO But is there any?

ISABELLA Yes, brother, you may live:
  There is a devilish mercy in the judge,
  If you'll implore it, that will free your life,
  But fetter you till death.

CLAUDIO Perpetual durance?

ISABELLA Ay, just; perpetual durance, a restraint,
  Though all the world's vastidity you had,
  To a determin'd scope.

CLAUDIO But in what nature?

ISABELLA In such a one as, you consenting to't,
  Would bark your honour from that trunk you bear,
  And leave you naked.

CLAUDIO Let me know the point.

ISABELLA O, I do fear thee, Claudio; and I quake,
  Lest thou a feverous life shouldst entertain,
  And six or seven winters more respect
  Than a perpetual honour. Dar'st thou die?
  The sense of death is most in apprehension;
  And the poor beetle that we tread upon
  In corporal sufferance finds a pang as great
  As when a giant dies.

CLAUDIO Why give you me this shame?
  Think you I can a resolution fetch
  From flow'ry tenderness? If I must die,
  I will encounter darkness as a bride
  And hug it in mine arms.

ISABELLA There spake my brother; there my father's grave
  Do utter forth a voice. Yes, thou must die:
  Thou art too noble to conserve a life
  In base appliances. This outward-sainted deputy,
  Whose settled visage and deliberate word
  Nips youth i' th' head, and follies doth enew
  As falcon doth the fowl, is yet a devil;
  His filth within being cast, he would appear
  A pond as deep as hell.

CLAUDIO The precise Angelo!

ISABELLA O, 'tis the cunning livery of hell
  The damned'st body to invest and cover
  In precise guards! Dost thou think, Claudio,
  If I would yield him my virginity
  Thou mightst be freed?

CLAUDIO O heavens! It cannot be.

ISABELLA Yes, he would give't thee, from this rank offence,
  So to offend him still. This night's the time
  That I should do what I abhor to name,
  Or else thou diest to-morrow.

CLAUDIO Thou shalt not do't.

ISABELLA O, were it but my life!
  I'd throw it down for your deliverance
  As frankly as a pin.

CLAUDIO Thanks, dear Isabel.

ISABELLA Be ready, Claudio, for your death to-morrow.

CLAUDIO Yes. Has he affections in him
  That thus can make him bite the law by th' nose
  When he would force it? Sure it is no sin;
  Or of the deadly seven it is the least.

ISABELLA Which is the least?

CLAUDIO If it were damnable, he being so wise,
  Why would he for the momentary trick
  Be perdurably fin'd? – O Isabel!

ISABELLA What says my brother?

CLAUDIO Death is a fearful thing.

ISABELLA And shamed life a hateful.

CLAUDIO Ay, but to die, and go we know not where;
  To lie in cold obstruction, and to rot;
  This sensible warm motion to become
  A kneaded clod; and the delighted spirit
  To bathe in fiery floods or to reside
  In thrilling region of thick-ribbed ice;
  To be imprison'd in the viewless winds,
  And blown with restless violence round about
  The pendent world; or to be worse than worst
  Of those that lawless and incertain thought
  Imagine howling – 'tis too horrible.
  The weariest and most loathed worldly life
  That age, ache, penury, and imprisonment,
  Can lay on nature is a paradise
  To what we fear of death.

ISABELLA Alas, alas!

CLAUDIO Sweet sister, let me live.
  What sin you do to save a brother's life,
  Nature dispenses with the deed so far
  That it becomes a virtue.

ISABELLA O you beast!
  O faithless coward! O dishonest wretch!
  Wilt thou be made a man out of my vice?
  Is't not a kind of incest to take life
  From thine own sister's shame? What should I think?
  Heaven shield my mother play'd my father fair!
  For such a warped slip of wilderness
  Ne'er issu'd from his blood. Take my defiance;
  Die; perish. Might but my bending down
  Reprieve thee from thy fate, it should proceed.
  I'll pray a thousand prayers for thy death,
  No word to save thee.
CLAUDIO Nay, hear me, Isabel.
ISABELLA O fie, fie, fie!
  Thy sin's not accidental, but a trade.
  Mercy to thee would prove itself a bawd;
  'Tis best that thou diest quickly.

DEREK   MARY MOONEY
late teens   15/16

Once a Catholic
Mary O'Malley

First performed at the Royal Court Theatre, London in 1977.

The play is set in the Convent of Our Lady of Fatima (a Grammar School for Girls), and in and around the streets of Willesden and Harlesden, London NW10 from September 1956 to July 1957.

Derek is a tall thin Teddy Boy in his late teens. He has been going out with Mary McGinty, a fifth former from the convent, for two and a half weeks. Now Mary McGinty has gone away to Fatima with the school and in this scene he turns his attention to the gullible Mary Mooney, also a fifth former and a friend of Mary McGinty's.

In this street scene, Mary Mooney is on her way to the library as Derek comes swaggering along in the opposite direction. They pass each other and Mary calls out to him.

Published by Amber Lane Press, Oxford

Act One, Scene Seventeen

MARY MOONEY Hello, Derek.

DEREK Eh? [*He stops and turns round.*] Er ... do I know you, darling?

MARY MOONEY Not really. But I was with Mary McGinty that day you met her along the street near our school.

DEREK Oh yeah?

MARY MOONEY You probably won't remember me but I'm Mary Mooney. There was another Mary with us as well that day. Mary Gallagher.

DEREK Oh, really?

MARY MOONEY Yes. You asked Mary McGinty if she'd meet you outside the White Hart that night. D'you remember?

DEREK Er ... vaguely. Bit of a long time ago, wasn't it?

144

MARY MOONEY The beginning of last term. But I've got a good memory for faces.

DEREK Oh, have you?

MARY MOONEY Yes.

DEREK Well, you'll have to excuse me not recognising you, darling. I mean, in them uniforms you all look like peas in a bleedin' pod. Seeing you all dressed up the way you are today, I wouldn't lump you in with none of them Lady of Fatima girls, now would I? Here, why ain't you in Fatima?

MARY MOONEY I didn't want to go.

DEREK Very wise, darling. Very wise. They're having a diabolical time, you know. I had a postcard Tuesday. She's got corns coming up on her kneecaps from having to say so many prayers. They have to be in bed by nine o'clock every night. And they have to go marching about all over the place in a crocodile. [*He laughs.*] I bet you're glad you stopped in Willesden, ain't you? [*He laughs.*] I hear they carted a midget along with 'em.

MARY MOONEY Oh, you mean Mary Finnegan in 5B. She's only as big as this. [*She holds her hand up about three feet in the air.*]

DEREK Gonna be coming back as big as this, is she? [*He holds his hand up about six feet in the air.*]

MARY MOONEY They're hoping she'll grow a bit bigger.

DEREK She won't, you know. She'll be coming back as little as what she went. You wait and see.

MARY MOONEY They won't be back for nearly another week.

DEREK Yeah, I know. Poor sods. Here, turn your face to the side a minute. D'you know who you remind me of?

MARY MOONEY Who?

DEREK Rhonda Fleming.

MARY MOONEY I don't.

DEREK Yes you do. I see her in a film last Saturday. Yeah, you're definitely her double, you are.

MARY MOONEY Am I?

DEREK I'm telling you. Er . . . d'you fancy coming for a bag of chips?

MARY MOONEY I've just had my dinner.

DEREK Oh. Well how about a cup of tea then?

MARY MOONEY I don't drink tea.

DEREK Well what do you drink?

MARY MOONEY Milk. Or water, or . . .

DEREK What, holy water?

MARY MOONEY Oooh, no.

DEREK Don't look so serious, darling. They can probably do you a glass of whatever you happen to fancy round the caff.

MARY MOONEY Well, actually, I was just on my way to the library.

DEREK Yeah? [*He takes one of the books from under her arm.*] What's this? *The Keys of the Kingdom*, eh? Do a lot of reading do you, darling?

MARY MOONEY There's not much else to do during the holidays.

DEREK What's this one all about then?

MARY MOONEY It's about a Catholic priest. Father Chisholm. He's a missionary and he goes out to China and . . .

DEREK Sounds highly intriguing I must say. Of course, I don't go in for reading much myself. No. I'd sooner watch the old TV.

MARY MOONEY So would I if we had one. But we haven't.

DEREK Ain't you? Oh well, you'll have to come round my house some time and have a watch of mine. Come round this afternoon if you like.

MARY MOONEY Oh, I don't know.

DEREK You're more than welcome, darling. I'm not doing nothing special this afternoon. I would have gone in to work but I had such a diabolical neuralgia this morning I couldn't lift me head off of the pillow. You gonna come then?

MARY MOONEY D'you really want me to?

DEREK I wouldn't ask you, would I?

MARY MOONEY All right then. I suppose I can always go to the library another day.

DEREK Course you can. Come on then, Rhonda. Let's go and get the bus.

PEGEEN	CHRISTY MAHON
young	young
Irish/West	Irish/West

The Playboy of the Western World
J.M. Synge

First produced at the Abbey Theatre, Dublin in 1907.

The action takes place near a village on the wild coast of Mayo. Christy Mahon, a young farmhand, has quarrelled with his father, striking the old man down and leaving him for dead. Terrified, he runs away and takes refuge in a country pub, or 'shebeen', run by Michael James and his daughter, Pegeen. Soon he comes to realise that a man who has killed his father is something of a curiosity amongst the locals – even a hero to the village girls, and in particular, the landlord's daughter. Now Christy has won the mule race and carried away all the prizes at the Sports.

In this scene he returns from his triumph, still dressed in his jockey suit. He is welcomed by a radiant Pegeen who, having shooed the crowd away from the door, begins to wipe his face with her shawl.

Published by A&C Black, London

Act Three

PEGEEN [*radiantly, wiping his face with her shawl*] Well, you're the lad, and you'll have great times from this out when you could win that wealth of prizes, and you sweating in the heat of noon!

CHRISTY [*looking at her with delight*] I'll have great times if I win the crowning prize I'm seeking now, and that's your promise that you'll wed me in a fortnight, when our banns is called.

PEGEEN [*backing away from him*] You've right daring to go ask me that, when all knows you'll be starting to some girl in your own townland, when your father's rotten in four months, or five.

CHRISTY [*indignantly*] Starting from you, is it? [*He follows her.*] I will not, then, and when the airs is warming in four months, or five, it's then yourself and me should be pacing Neifin in the dews of night, the times sweet smells do be rising, and you'd see a little, shiny new moon, maybe, sinking on the hills.

PEGEEN [*looking at him playfully*] And it's that kind of a poacher's love you'd make, Christy Mahon, on the sides of Neifin, when the night is down?

CHRISTY It's little you'll think if my love's a poacher's, or an earl's itself, when you'll feel my two hands stretched around you, and I squeezing kisses on your puckered lips, till I'd feel a kind of pity for the Lord God is all ages sitting lonesome in his golden chair.

PEGEEN That'll be right fun, Christy Mahon, and any girl would walk her heart out before she'd meet a young man was your like for eloquence, or talk, at all.

CHRISTY [*encouraged*] Let you wait, to hear me talking, till we're astray in Erris, when Good Friday's by, drinking a sup from a well, and making mighty kisses with our wetted mouths, or gaming in a gap of sunshine, with yourself stretched back unto your necklace, in the flowers of the earth.

PEGEEN [*in a lower voice, moved by his tone*] I'd be nice so, is it?

CHRISTY [*with rapture*] If the mitred bishops seen you that time, they'd be the like of the holy prophets, I'm thinking, do be straining the bars of Paradise to lay eyes on the Lady Helen of Troy, and she abroad, pacing back and forward, with a nosegay in her golden shawl.

PEGEEN [*with real tenderness*] And what is I have, Christy Mahon, to make me fitting entertainment for the like of you, that has such poet's talking, and such bravery of heart?

CHRISTY [*in a low voice*] Isn't there the light of seven heavens in your heart alone, the way you'll be an angel's lamp to me from this out, and I abroad in the darkness, spearing salmons in the Owen, or the Carrowmore?

PEGEEN If I was your wife, I'd be along with you those nights, Christy Mahon, the way you'd see I was a great hand at coaxing bailiffs, or coining funny nick-names for the stars of night.

CHRISTY You, is it? Taking your death in the hailstones, or the fogs of dawn.

PEGEEN Yourself and me would shelter easy in a narrow bush, [*with a qualm of dread*] but we're only talking, maybe, for this would be a poor, thatched place to hold a fine lad is the like of you.

CHRISTY [*putting his arm round her*] If I wasn't a good Christian, it's on my naked knees I'd be saying my prayers and paters to every jackstraw you have roofing your head, and every stony pebble is paving the laneway to your door.

PEGEEN [*radiantly*] If that's the truth, I'll be burning candles from this out to the miracles of God have brought you from the south today, and I, with my gowns bought ready, the way that I can wed you, and not wait at all.

CHRISTY It's miracles, and that's the truth. Me there toiling a long while, and walking a long while, not knowing at all I was drawing all times nearer to this holy day.

PEGEEN And myself, a girl, was tempted often to go sailing the seas till I'd marry a Jew-man, with ten kegs of gold, and I not knowing at all there was the like of you drawing nearer, like the stars of God.

CHRISTY And to think I'm long years hearing women talking that talk, to all bloody fools, and this the first time I've heard the like of your voice talking sweetly for my own delight.

PEGEEN And to think it's me is talking sweetly, Christy Mahon, and I the fright of seven townlands for my biting tongue. Well, the heart's a wonder; and, I'm thinking, there won't be our like in Mayo, for gallant lovers, from this hour, today. [*Drunken singing is heard outside.*] There's my father coming from the wake, and when he's had his sleep we'll tell him, for he's peaceful then.

MRS BENNET
middle-aged

MR BENNET
middle-aged

Pride and Prejudice

Jane Austen
Adapted for stage by Sue Pomeroy

First performed at the Key Theatre, Peterborough by Good Company in September 1995 as part of a 28-week tour, finishing at the Theatre Royal, Bath in June 1996.

When a young, single man of large fortune comes to live in the neighbourhood, Mrs Bennet is determined that he shall marry one of her daughters, in spite of her husband's apparent indifference to such matters.

Set in Regency England, in the Hertfordshire village of Longbourn, this opening scene takes place in Mr Bennet's sanctuary, his library. Lost in his reading, he is suddenly interrupted by his wife bursting in with news of such vital importance to her that it cannot wait.

Act One, Scene One

MRS BENNET Mr Bennet! Such news! I cannot wait a moment longer. [*As he attempts to ignore her.*] No sir – I must interrupt you!

MR BENNET Ever of an impetuous nature my dear.

MRS BENNET Netherfield Park is let at last! Mrs Long has told me all about it!

MR BENNET Ah! [*Replaces a book in the shelves.*]

MRS BENNET Do you not want to know who has taken it?

MR BENNET If you must tell me, my dear, I have no objection to listening.

MRS BENNET [*conspiratorially*] Netherfield has been taken by a young man, and with a large fortune. He is to take possession by the end of the month!

MR BENNET What is his name?

MRS BENNET Bingley.

MR BENNET Is he married or single?

MRS BENNET Single of course! A single man, with four or five
thousand a year! What a fine thing for our girls!

MR BENNET Indeed? [*Takes out book and inspects it.*]

MRS BENNET My dear Mr Bennet. How can you be so tiresome!
You must know that I am thinking of him marrying one of
them.

MR BENNET [*a moment*] Is that his design in settling here?

MRS BENNET What nonsense, what makes you talk so! There is
every reason to expect that he will fall in love at least with
one of them. My dear, you must go and pay our respects to
Mr Bingley as soon as he is moved in.

MR BENNET I see no occasion for that. But you go with the girls
– certainly you are as handsome as they – indeed Mr Bingley
may like you the best of the party.

MRS BENNET You flatter me Mr Bennet. I have once been considered something of a beauty, but alas I no longer turn heads as
once I used to. No, time and duty are a woman's greatest
enemies. A woman with five grown up daughters must forsake
thinking of her own beauty.

MR BENNET Indeed in such a case a woman has often not much
beauty left to think of.

MRS BENNET [*ignoring him and returning to the main matter*]
No, it will be impossible for *us* to visit Mr Bingley if you do
not.

MR BENNET I have a better idea – I will write him a letter, which
you may present to him on his arrival, to assure him he has my
hearty consent to marry whichever of my daughters he chooses.

MRS BENNET How can you be so whimsical Mr Bennet? You
surely know as well as I how all depends on a good match for
our girls. Mr Bingley will be the principal batchelor in the
neighbourhood and I am by no means the first to think it.
What will happen if you will not bestir yourself? Your daughters will be beaten to any prospects of rich husbands, we all
shall be destitute, and poverty will be your only legacy.

MR BENNET My dear, could I have tried harder to secure our
future by obtaining a male heir for the estate? I have bestirred
myself often enough I believe, and have been provided with a
daughter on each occasion. However if you are of a mind that
providence will smile upon us this time, I have not forgot the
way to your chamber and will bestir myself again.

MRS BENNET Mr Bennet, you take delight in vexing me. You have
no compassion on my poor nerves.

MR BENNET On the contrary my dear. I have a healthy respect for your nerves. They have been my constant companions for the past twenty years.

MRS BENNET You have no idea what I go through!

MR BENNET Perhaps not my dear, but I am sure you will get over it and live to see many young men of such good prospects move into the neighbourhood.

MRS BENNET And much good may that do us, if you will not visit any of them! [*Exits.*]

MR BENNET [*tetchily*] In a household of six women, I do make it a rule to have peace in my library.

LUCY
young

SIR LUCIUS O'TRIGGER
middle-aged
Irish

The Rivals

Richard Brinsley Sheridan

This eighteenth-century Comedy of Manners was first performed at the Theatre Royal, Covent Garden in 1775.

The play is set in Bath and revolves around the rivals for the hand of the lovely Lydia Languish and the subsequent intrigues leading up to a comic attempt at a duel, arranged by Sir Lucius O'Trigger, a penniless Irish baronet. Meanwhile, Lydia's middle-aged aunt, Mrs Malaprop, has developed a passion for Sir Lucius and is sending him love letters via her unscrupulous maid, Lucy, who has persuaded the baronet that he is corresponding not with the aunt, but with the niece.

In this scene, Lucy brings Sir Lucius the latest letter from his 'dear Dalia', making sure that she receives her usual reward.

Published by A&C Black, London

Act Two, Scene Two

LUCY So – I shall have another rival to add to my mistress's list – Captain Absolute. – However, I shall not enter his name till my purse has received notice in form[1]. Poor Acres is dismissed! Well, I have done him a last friendly office, in letting him know that Beverley was here before him. Sir Lucius is generally more punctual when he expects to hear from his *dear Dalia*, as he calls her: I wonder he's not here! I have a little scruple of conscience from this deceit; though I should not be paid so well, if my hero knew that Delia was near fifty, and her own mistress. [*Enter Sir Lucius O'Trigger.*]

SIR LUCIUS Hah! my little embassadress – upon my conscience I have been looking for you; I have been on the South Parade this half-hour.

LUCY [*speaking simply*] O gemini! and I have been waiting for your worship here on the North.

SIR LUCIUS Faith! – maybe that was the reason we did not meet; and it is very comical too, how you could go out and I not see you – for I was only taking a nap at the Parade coffee-house, and I chose the window on purpose that I might not miss you.

LUCY My stars! Now I'd wager a sixpence I went by while you were asleep.

SIR LUCIUS Sure enough it must have been so – and I never dreamt it was so late, till I waked. Well, but my little girl, have you got nothing for me?

LUCY Yes, but I have – I've got a letter for you in my pocket.

SIR LUCIUS O faith! I guessed you weren't come up empty-handed – well – let me see what the dear creature says.

LUCY There, Sir Lucius. [*Gives him a letter.*]

SIR LUCIUS [*reads*] *Sir – there is often a sudden incentive[2] impulse in love, that has a greater induction[3] than years of domestic combination: such was the commotion[4] I felt at the first super-fluous[5] view of Sir Lucius O'Trigger.* Very pretty, upon my word. *Female punctuation[6] forbids me to say more; yet let me add, that it will give me joy infallible[7] to find Sir Lucius worthy the last criterion of my affections. – Delia.* Upon my conscience! Lucy, your lady is a great mistress of language. Faith, she's quite the queen of the dictionary! – for the devil a word dare refuse coming at her call – though one would think it was quite out of hearing.

LUCY Aye, Sir, a lady of her experience.

SIR LUCIUS Experience! What, at seventeen?

LUCY O true, Sir – but then she reads so – my stars! How she will read off-hand[8]!

SIR LUCIUS Faith, she must be very deep read to write this way – though she is a rather arbitrary writer too – for here are a great many poor words pressed[9] into the service of this note, that would get their *habeas corpus* from any court in Christendom. – However, when affection guides the pen, Lucy, he must be a brute who finds fault with the style.

LUCY Ah! Sir Lucius, if you were to hear how she talks of you!

SIR LUCIUS O tell her, I'll make her the best husband in the world, and Lady O'Trigger into the bargain! But we must get the old gentlewoman's consent – and do everything fairly.

LUCY Nay, Sir Lucius, I thought you wa'n't rich enough to be so nice[10]!

SIR LUCIUS Upon my word, young woman, you have hit it: I am so poor that I can't afford to do a dirty action. If I did not want money I'd steal your mistress and her fortune with a great deal of pleasure. – However, my pretty girl, [*gives her money*] here's a little something to buy you a riband; and meet me in the evening, and I'll give you an answer to this. So, hussy, take a kiss beforehand, to put you in mind.
[*Kisses her.*]

LUCY O Lud! Sir Lucius – I never seed such a gemman! My lady won't like you if you're so impudent.

SIR LUCIUS Faith she will, Lucy – that same – pho! what's the name of it? – modesty! – is a quality in a lover more praised by the women than liked; so, if your mistress asks you whether Sir Lucius ever gave you a kiss, tell her *fifty* – my dear.

LUCY What, would you have me tell her a lie?

SIR LUCIUS Ah then, you baggage! I'll make it a truth presently[11].

LUCY For shame now; here is someone coming.

SIR LUCIUS O faith, I'll quiet your conscience.

[1]*in form* according to the prescribed method (i.e., by bribing her)

[2]*incentive* provocative, arousing

[3]*induction* in a strained sense, an introductory process; or for, inducement

[4]*commotion* for, emotion?

[5]*superfluous* for, superficial

[6]*punctuation* for, punctilio

[7]*infallible* possibly in the sense of 'certain'; or for, ineffable

[8]*off-hand* straight off

[9]*pressed* forcibly enlisted, as by the press-gang

[10]*nice* particular, fastidious, scrupulous

[11]*presently* without delay

KEITH
20s

VIVIAN
20s

Spend, Spend, Spend
Jack Rosenthal

Produced for television in 1977, the play is a dramatisation of a true story of two young pools winners from Yorkshire, Keith and Vivian Nicholson, to whom the money only brought boredom, isolation and tragedy. After the presentation cere-mony at the Grosvenor Hotel in 1961, Vivian is asked what she intends to do with all that money. She replies, 'I'm going to spend, spend, spend!!'

This scene takes place that night in their luxury bedroom where Vivian has already covered the bedside table with bottles of expensive liqueurs. She is wearing a black bra and panties and is stone cold sober and furious. As Keith comes into the room dressed in brand-new clothes and merrily tipsy, she deals him a hefty smack in the face.

Published by Penguin Plays, London

Scene Eleven

KEITH What the hell's that for???

VIVIAN If that's what money does for you, I'll burn the bugger!

KEITH What money? I've only had it half a sodding day!

VIVIAN Showing me up . . .

KEITH What doing?

VIVIAN *You* know.

KEITH I don't!

VIVIAN Well, *I* do!

[*She furiously continues doing what she was doing before he came in – polishing the mirrors.*
Keith watches her, puzzled.]

KEITH What are *you* doing?

[*She ignores him.*]

They have chambermaids for that . . .

VIVIAN I saw you, Keith Nicholson! Pegging up chorus-girls' legs
... eyes stuck out like chapel hat-pegs.

KEITH When?

VIVIAN 'When?', he says! Tonight! With half the sodding
Palladium watching you!

KEITH I couldn't help myself, you daft bat! *We're* on the front
row, and *they're* kicking them in the air! What were I supposed
to do – shut my eyes?

VIVIAN You didn't gawp at Sammy Davis like that ...

[*Keith laughs. Sits on the edge of the bed, taking his shoes off.*]

KEITH *All* the fellers were looking, love ... all the Littlewoods
lot ... I did nowt wrong.

VIVIAN I'd have gouged your eyes *out*, if you had!

[*She continues polishing the mirrors.*
Keith starts undressing, still watching her, puzzled.]

KEITH I wish I knew what the hell you were doing!

VIVIAN What's it look like?

KEITH What's it *for*?

[*She turns to face him, smiles sexily and comes towards him.*
She puts her arms round his waist.]

VIVIAN [*quietly, sexily*] We're rich now, lover-boy. We can do
anything we want. We can lie in bed and rub pound notes all
over each other. A hundred and fifty thousand of them ...

KEITH [*laughs*] We'd have a job! It's in a cheque.

VIVIAN We'll cash it.

KEITH The bank's got it.

VIVIAN We'll draw it out.

KEITH They're shut.

[*The above five speeches are said smilingly, teasingly – a sort
of gentle sexual foreplay.*]

VIVIAN Fair do's. We'll pour Dubonnet over each other instead.
[*Smiles.*] Then lick it off.

KEITH [*half amused, half excited*] Is that right?

[*She nods towards the bedside table. It's covered with bottles
of liqueurs.*]

VIVIAN I've got them in ready.

KEITH [*looking*] Crikey! How much did that lot come to?

VIVIAN [*grins*] Who cares?

[*They move into a close embrace.*]

KEITH I still don't know what the mirrors are for ...

VIVIAN All the better to see you with.

KEITH What doing?

VIVIAN With our money, we can afford a good view ...
[*She promptly starts tearing his clothes off, laughing, then grabs bottles and starts pouring their contents over his bared chest. Pan away from them, round the room, which is littered with a mass of expensively wrapped purchases.*
Over this:]

VIVIAN [*O.O.V.*] We'll have the best sexual happening of all time ...

KEITH [*O.O.V.*] The best what??

VIVIAN [*O.O.V.*] You heard.

KEITH [*O.O.V.*] That's not what *I* call it.

VIVIAN Dirty sod ...

MR CHERRY OWEN
Welsh

MRS CHERRY OWEN
Welsh

Under Milk Wood
Dylan Thomas

A play for voices first broadcast by the BBC in 1954 and presented on stage at the Edinburgh Festival in 1956.

The setting is a small Welsh town one night in spring, when all the inhabitants lie sleeping and dreaming their own particular dreams. The action continues as they wake up and go about their day's work and on through to the evening when they begin to settle down and go to sleep again. The scenes are linked by the 'Voices'.

A cock crows, the town awakes and breakfasts are put on pans. This scene between Mr Cherry Owen and Mrs Cherry Owen is introduced by First Voice. The use of First Voice is optional and can be played by either of the two actors as an introduction to the scene, or by a presenter.

Published by Everyman Classics, The Orion Publishing Group Ltd.

[FIRST VOICE Mr and Mrs Cherry Owen, in their Donkey Street room that is bedroom, parlour, kitchen, and scullery, sit down to last night's supper of onions boiled in their overcoats and broth of spuds and baconrind and leeks and bones.]

MRS CHERRY OWEN See that smudge on the wall by the picture of Auntie Blossom? That's where you threw the sago.
  [*Cherry Owen laughs with delight.*]
MRS CHERRY OWEN You only missed me by an inch.
CHERRY OWEN I always miss Auntie Blossom too.
MRS CHERRY OWEN Remember last night? In you reeled, my boy, as drunk as a deacon with a big wet bucket and a fish-frail full of stout and you looked at me and you said, 'God has come home!' you said, and then over the bucket you went, sprawling and bawling, and the floor was all flagons and eels.

CHERRY OWEN Was I wounded?

MRS CHERRY OWEN And then you took off your trousers and you said, 'Does anybody want a fight!' Oh, you old baboon.

CHERRY OWEN Give me a kiss.

MRS CHERRY OWEN And then you sang 'Bread of Heaven', tenor and bass.

CHERRY OWEN I *always* sing 'Bread of Heaven'.

MRS CHERRY OWEN And then you did a little dance on the table.

CHERRY OWEN I did?

MRS CHERRY OWEN Drop dead!

CHERRY OWEN And then what did I do?

MRS CHERRY OWEN Then you cried like a baby and said you were a poor drunk orphan with nowhere to go but the grave.

CHERRY OWEN And what did I do next, my dear?

MRS CHERRY OWEN Then you danced on the table all over again and said you were King Solomon Owen and I was your Mrs Sheba.

CHERRY OWEN [*softly*] And then?

MRS CHERRY OWEN And then I got you into bed and you snored all night like a brewery.

[*Mr and Mrs Cherry Owen laugh delightedly together.*]

RUBY BIRTLE
very young
Yorkshire accent

GERALD FORBES
young

When We Are Married
J.B. Priestley

First performed at St Martin's Theatre, London in 1938, and described as a Yorkshire farcical comedy.

The action takes place in the sitting-room of Alderman Helliwell's house in Clecklewyke, a town in the West Riding, on an evening in 1908. Twenty-five years ago the Helliwells, the Parkers and the Soppitts were married – all on the same day and by the same parson. Now they have gathered to celebrate their silver wedding.

In this opening scene, Ruby Birtle, a young 'slavey' of the period, shows young Gerald Forbes into the sitting-room. Gerald, unlike Ruby and most of the other characters, does not talk with a West Riding accent. He is organist and choirmaster of the local chapel and has an appointment to see Alderman Halliwell.

Published by Samuel French, London

Act One
RUBY You'll have to wait, 'cos they haven't finished their tea.
GERALD Bit late, aren't they?
RUBY [*approaching, confidentially*] It's a do.
GERALD It's what?
RUBY A do. Y'know, they've company.
GERALD Oh – I see. It's a sort of party, and they're having high tea.
RUBY [*after nodding, going closer still*] Roast pork, stand pie, salmon and salad, trifle, two kinds o' jellies, lemon-cheese tarts, jam tarts, swiss tarts, sponge cake, walnut cake, chocolate roll, and a pound cake kept from last Christmas.
GERALD [*with irony*] Is that all?
RUBY [*seriously*] No, there's white bread, brown bread, currant

161

teacake, one o' them big curd tarts from Gregory's, and a lot
o' cheese.

GERALD It *is* a do, isn't it?

RUBY [*after nodding, then very confidentially*] *And* a little brown
jug.

GERALD [*turning, astonished*] A little brown jug?

RUBY [*still confidentially*] You know what that is, don't you?
Don't you? [*She laughs.*] Well, I never did! Little brown jug's
a drop o' rum for your tea. They're getting right lively on it.
[*Coolly.*] But you don't come from round here, do you?

GERALD [*not disposed for a chat*] No.

[*A distant bell rings, not the front-door bell.*]

RUBY I come from near Rotherham. Me father works in t'pit,
and so does our Frank and our Wilfred.

[*The distant bell sounds again.*]

GERALD There's a bell ringing somewhere.

RUBY [*coolly*] I know. It's for me. Let her wait. She's run me off
me legs to-day. And Mrs Northrop's in t'kitchen – she can do
a bit for a change. [*She crosses to Gerald.*] There's seven of
'em at it in t'dining-room – Alderman Helliwell and missus,
of course – then Councillor Albert Parker and Mrs Parker, and
Mr Herbert Soppitt and Mrs Soppitt – and of course Miss
Holmes.

GERALD Oh – Miss Holmes *is* there, is she?

RUBY Yes, but she's stopped eating. [*She giggles.*] You're courting
her, aren't you?

GERALD [*astonished and alarmed*] What!

RUBY [*coolly*] Oh – I saw you both – the other night, near Cleckley
Woods. I was out meself, with our milkman's lad.

[*Gerald turns away.*]

Now don't look like that, I won't tell on you.

GERALD [*producing a shilling, then rather desperately*] Now –
look here! What's your name?

RUBY Ruby Birtle.

GERALD Well, Ruby, you wouldn't like Miss Holmes to get into
a row here with her uncle and aunt, would you?

RUBY No, I wouldn't like that. But I'd like that shilling.

GERALD [*after giving it to her*] You said Miss Holmes had finished
eating.

RUBY Yes. She can't put it away like some of 'em. I'd rather keep
Councillor Albert Parker a week than a fortnight. D'you want
to see her?

GERALD Yes. Could you just give her the tip quietly that I'm here – if the rest of them aren't coming in here yet?

RUBY Not them! You'd think they'd been pined for a month – way they're going at it! [*She turns up stage.*] I'll tell her. [*She turns back.*] She'd better come round that way – through t'greenhouse—

Copyright Holders

The following have kindly granted permission to us to reproduce copyright material.

Another Country by Julian Mitchell
Published by Amber Lane Press. Reprinted by permission of Amber Lane Press.

Once a Catholic by Mary O'Malley
Published by Amber Lane Press. Reprinted by permission of Amber Lane Press.

Art by Yasmina Reza translated by Christopher Hampton
Published by Faber and Faber Ltd. Reprinted by permission of Faber and Faber Ltd.

On the Ledge by Alan Bleasdale
Published by Faber and Faber Ltd. Reprinted by permission of Faber and Faber Ltd.

Borderline by Hanif Kureishi
From *Outskirts and Other Plays* published by Faber and Faber Ltd. Reprinted by permission of Faber and Faber Ltd.

Dirty Linen by Tom Stoppard
From *Dirty Linen and New-Found-Land* published by Faber and Faber Ltd. Reprinted by permission of Faber and Faber Ltd.

Indian Ink by Tom Stoppard
Published by Faber and Faber Ltd. Reprinted by permission of Faber and Faber Ltd.

Les Liaisons Dangereuses translated and adapted by Christopher Hampton from the novel by Choderlos de Laclos
Published by Faber and Faber Ltd. Reprinted by permission of Faber and Faber Ltd.

The Positive Hour by April de Angelis
Published by Faber and Faber Ltd. Reprinted by permission of Faber and Faber Ltd.

Someone Who'll Watch Over Me by Frank McGuinness
Reproduced by permisson of Frank McGuinness, c/o The Agency (London) Ltd., 24 Pottery Lane, London W11 4LZ

Blood Knot by Athol Fugard
Taken from *The Blood Knot* by Athol Fugard, by permission of Oxford University Press.

Sleuth by Anthony Shaffer
Reprinted by permission of The Peters Fraser and Dunlop Group Limited on behalf of: Anthony Shaffer Copyright © 1970 by Peter Shaffer Limited.

Green Forms by Alan Bennett
Reprinted by permission of The Peters Fraser and Dunlop Group Limited on behalf of: Alan Bennett Copyright © 1981 by Alan Bennett.

When We Are Married by J.B. Priestley
Reprinted by permission of The Peters Fraser and Dunlop Group Limited on behalf of: J.B. Priestley Copyright © 1938 J.B. Priestley.

Plunder by Ben Travers
Reprinted by permission of The Peters Fraser and Dunlop Group Limited on behalf of: The Estate of Ben Travers Copyright © Ben Travers 1928.

Stevie by Hugh Whitemore
Reprinted by permission of Amber Lane Press. Copyright © Hugh Whitemore Ltd 1977.

Dead Dad Dog by John McKay
From *Scot-Free: New Scottish Plays* published by Nick Hern Books. Reprinted by permission of Nick Hern Books.

Kindertransport by Diane Samuels
Published by Nick Hern Books. Reprinted by permission of Nick Hern Books.

The Steamie by Tony Roper
From *Scot-Free: New Scottish Plays* published by Nick Hern Books. Reprinted by permission of Nick Hern Books.

The Herbal Bed by Peter Whelan
Copyright © 1996 by Peter Whelan. Reprinted by permission of Warner/Chappell Plays Limited. All rights reserved.

Up 'n' Under by John Godber
Pages 116–20 from *Up 'n' Under* in 'Five Plays' by John Godber (Penguin Books, 1989) Copyright © John Godber, 1985, 1989. Reproduced by permission of Frederick Warne & Co.

Amadeus by Peter Shaffer
Pages 90–3 from *Amadeus* by Peter Shaffer (Penguin Books, 1981) Copyright © Peter Shaffer, 1980, 1981. Reproduced by permission of Frederick Warne & Co.

Back to Methusaleh by Bernard Shaw
From *The Collected Plays with their prefaces*, Bernard Shaw, published by The Bodley Head. Reprinted by permission of The Society of Authors on behalf of the Bernard Shaw Estate.

Bold Girls by Rona Munro
Published by Hodder and Stoughton. Reprinted by permission of Hodder and Stoughton Ltd.

Have You Seen Zandile? by Gcina Mhlope, Maralin Vanrenen and Thiembi Mtshalii
Reprinted by permission of Gcina Mhlope, Maralin Vanrenen and Thiembe Mtshalii: *Have You Seen Zandile?* (Heinemann, A Division of Reed Elsevier Inc., Portsmouth, NH, 1988).

An Echo in the Bone by Dennis Scott
Reprinted with permission of Joy R. Scott.

Pride and Prejudice stage adaptation by Sue Pomeroy
Reprinted by permission of Sue Pomeroy.

Under Milk Wood by Dylan Thomas
Published by Everyman Classics, The Orion Publishing Group Ltd.